The Invisible Man

A self-help guide for men with eating disorders, compulsive exercising and bigorexia

John F. Morgan

Routledge
Taylor & Francis Group

LONDON AND NEW YORK

First published 2008 by Routledge
27 Church Road, Hove, East Sussex BN3 2FA

Simultaneously published in the USA and Canada
by Routledge
270 Madison Avenue, New York, NY 10016

Routledge is an imprint of the Taylor & Francis Group, an Informa Business

© 2008 John F. Morgan

Typeset in Times by Garfield Morgan, Swansea, West Glamorgan
Printed and bound in Great Britain by TJ International Ltd, Padstow, Cornwall
Paperback cover design by Sandra Heath

This publication has been produced with paper manufactured to strict
environmental standards and with pulp derived from sustainable forests.

British Library Cataloguing in Publication Data
A catalogue record for this book is available from the British Library

Library of Congress Cataloging-in-Publication Data
Morgan, John F., 1966–
    The invisible man : a self-help guide for men with eating disorders,
compulsive exercise and bigorexia / John F. Morgan.
        p. cm.
    Includes bibliographical references and index.
    ISBN 978-1-58391-149-5 (hardback) – ISBN 978-1-58391-150-1 (pbk.) 1.
Eating disorders in men. 2. Body image in men. I. Title.
    RC552.E18M67 2008
    616.85'260081–dc22

                                                        2007037632

ISBN: 978-1-58391-149-5 (hbk)
ISBN: 978-1-58391-150-1 (pbk)

Contents

Illustrations

Figures

Tables

Boxes

Foreword

Almost all previous books on anorexia nervosa and bulimia nervosa have been written for the female reader. The effect on the large number of male sufferers has been understandable. It has, to men, become the illness that may not speak its name. It is, they reason, bad enough to have anorexia without everyone thinking you have a woman's disorder.

John Morgan is one of the foremost clinicians in eating disorders in the United Kingdom. He is a researcher whose influence reaches internationally. Dr Morgan has recognised that men with eating disorders have particular needs and he addresses these in this excellent book. He has brought theory and practice together to develop a seamless approach which is cogent and powerful.

As Dr Morgan writes, the book has been written for all those "invisible men who have been neglected and stigmatised". He has done this by starting afresh. Here, there is none of the preoccupation with women's social issues, femininity and the like, with the issues of men subsumed in a brief paragraph. Rather, Dr Morgan bases his treatment on the modern man in society. There is a basis to the burgeoning prevalence of the disorder in men and understanding it is half the battle. He explains in clear terms the sociology and science which underpin the disorders. All sufferers will recognise themselves and be reassured.

The second strength of the book is that it provides a practical and comprehensive self-help treatment approach, which is not a variant of that offered to women but especially tailored for men. The treatment can either be used for recovery in its own right, or for the man or boy to prepare himself for professional help, or to maintain success that has been achieved by other means.

This book has been written in a lucid style and provides a carefully-structured guideline to health. It can be warmly commended.

Professor J Hubert Lacey
Professor of Psychiatry
St George's, University of London & Lead Clinician,
St George's Eating Disorders Service

Preface

There is a rising problem of boys and men with eating disorders and related body image problems. Some may have full-blown conditions such as anorexia nervosa, bulimia, binge eating, compulsive exercising or bigorexia (muscle dysmorphia). Others are distressed by slightly lesser degrees of disordered eating or over-exercise, and seek ways of overcoming their problem.

At least one in ten people with eating disorders is a man or boy, and an even greater proportion of men have problems of compulsive exercise. Younger men are becoming more vulnerable to disliking their bodies, and seeking to artificially reshape them. This arises in the context of a broader crisis of masculinity. It is hard to read a newspaper these days without reports of 'feral youths'. Suddenly the role of 'the father' has become headline news. Many men don't quite know what the 'rules' are. Masculine attributes are rarely celebrated. Men lack the skills to discuss their feelings, and can rarely bring themselves to discuss their health, never mind issues of sexuality. It is unsurprising that so many young men are beginning to retreat into the toxic worlds of eating disorders and compulsive exercise.

The media have become obsessed with women's eating disorders. I give interviews at least once a month to magazines and newspapers about these matters. Governments have become sufficiently concerned to convene 'body image' summits and instigate 'codes of practice' for women's magazines. These are welcome moves, beyond reproach. But male eating disorders, compulsive exercise and body image disparagement receive little attention. Getting help can seem like an impossible task, and recognising you need help is often overwhelming. Sometimes it can feel like there are nothing but obstacles on the road to recovery, and it can feel like a very lonely road.

Yet *The Invisible Man* is written in a spirit of optimism. We have more scientific knowledge about men with eating disorders than ever before. In treatment, we know what works and what doesn't. In managing medical complications, we know the risks and the remedies.

The book is written for all those 'invisible men' who have been neglected and stigmatised, who have struggled to receive adequate treatment or have been received unsympathetically by health-care professionals who think that 'men don't get eating disorders'. I began to write the book five years ago while working at the St George's Eating Disorder Service in London, and finished it when I became head of the Yorkshire Centre for Eating Disorders in Leeds. During that time, the problem has got bigger and bigger, but so has our knowledge.

I also wrote *The Invisible Man* for all those relatives and friends of boys and men with eating disorders, who don't know what to do and would like a 'rule book'. This isn't a rule book, but it may help you understand why there are no rules.

I have written *The Invisible Man* in four parts. Part I paints a picture of the wider context in which men suffer body image problems. It looks at the detailed history of male eating disorders, challenging the idea that these are new conditions. It examines the barriers to recovery, or what has been described as a 'snakes and ladders' experience. Part II looks at the nature of the various conditions, including the features of anorexia nervosa, bulimia, binge eating, bigorexia (muscle dysmorphia) and obesity that are unique to men. Part III examines the science fact and science fiction, drawing on our research portfolio that has explored biological, psychological and social aspects of these disorders.

Part IV provides a practical, seven-stage approach to treatment. For some men, this may be sufficient to break the dreadful cycle of crooked thinking, bad habits and ambiguous feelings that often perpetuate eating and body image disorders. For most, *The Invisible Man* will be the beginning of a longer journey that might involve professional help. Men and boys with anorexia nervosa in particular will usually require therapy from an eating disorder service, and medical complications of eating disorders or muscle dysmorphia will require the input of an experienced specialist.

The practical 'homework' in *The Invisible Man* is designed to make things change. So reading the book won't be an easy or a passive experience. You will be asked to do things that will challenge you. For example, keeping a 'food diary' may irritate you. It is likely that you will feel like giving up at some point, and you may even need to work through *The Invisible Man* more than once. Your head will tell you that change is always difficult, but your heart may try to convince you that there is no need to change. Learning to distinguish healthy from unhealthy thoughts is part of the process of recovery.

It is hard to define what we mean by 'recovery', but it is generally better to judge yourself by what you 'do' rather than how you 'feel'. For example, weight gain is essential in recovery from anorexia nervosa, cessation of vomiting and purging is central to recovery in bulimia, and reduction in frequency of exercise is the yardstick of recovery in bigorexia. At the end of that process, you may harbour unresolved issues about body image or personal relationships. For some men, it can be enough to break the cycle of behaviours, and recovery can occur within months. For others, it is necessary to delve deeper and recovery can take years. But behavioural change is a necessary, if not always sufficient, part of that process. As you embark on this journey, you may feel worse before you feel better. If at any stage your emotions become overwhelming, you must seek professional help.

Most men with eating disorders or problems of compulsive exercise will recover. That is why *The Invisible Man* is optimistic. Often it is a question of putting several small pieces of the jigsaw together at the same time, before you can see the 'big picture', rather than waiting for a single, solitary revelation. *The Invisible Man* is designed to be one of those pieces, and the rest is up to you.

Note

All client names and details in the case vignettes have been changed throughout the book to protect identity.

Acknowledgements

My gratitude goes to Professor Hubert Lacey who has been at the forefront of innovative research into eating disorders throughout my career, and a kind mentor.

I have been inspired by the work of Beat, the UK's eating disorder association, to whom I donate some of *The Invisible Man*'s royalties.

I am indebted to staff at the Yorkshire Centre for Eating Disorders, who present a model of care which is unparalleled.

Finally, everything I know of eating disorders has been learned through dialogue with my patients, past and present.

Part I

Fat is more than a feminist issue

Chapter 1

Snakes and ladders

Barriers to recovery

Men with body image problems and eating disorders suffer tremendous physical and psychological distress. We know how to treat these illnesses and the remedies are quite effective. So why aren't men with eating disorders accessing treatment as readily as women? Although at least 10 per cent of people with eating disorders are men, a far lower proportion receives treatment from specialist eating disorder services. In some services, less than 1 per cent of their patients are men. What are the barriers to recovery?

This isn't easy to explain in simple terms. There appears to be a whole range of hurdles to overcome on the route from illness to recovery. One of my patients described it as 'like a game of snakes and ladders'.

Stigma

In the past, problems of the mind were seen as a sign of distinction and divine fury, closely allayed to creativity and genius. While science has brought humanity, understanding and hope to the treatment of these problems, including eating disorders and bigorexia, this has not broken down the barriers of stigmatisation.

Men with eating disorders and body image problems are particularly at risk of stigmatisation, not only from people around them but also from themselves. 'Men don't get eating disorders', 'you should put-up-and-shut-up', or 'real men don't cry', are examples of attitudes deeply embedded in our culture.

The inadequacy of treatment facilities for men with eating disorders or related body image problems is met not with a bang, but with a whimper. Research into 'male body image disorders' is a growth industry, but needs to be matched by provision of treatment services adapted to the needs of men. As long as body image is considered nothing but a 'feminist issue', doctors will continue to under-diagnose men with eating disorders, restrict their access to evidence-based treatment and fail in the management of gender-specific issues.

In 2000, the British government hosted a 'Body Image Summit' at Downing Street, attended by fashion magazine editors, advertisers, and teenage girls. They debated the way in which young girls' body image influenced their self-esteem, and the growth of eating disorders in young women. It was hosted by the government's 'Minister for Women' who called for a voluntary code of practice in the media. The meeting concluded with a call to 'smash the stereotypical images' of women.

It would be churlish to criticise the intent behind such a campaign. However, the outcome was to employ gender bias to an arena that transcends gender. There was neither representation nor discussion of issues of body image affecting men. Commitments from editors of women's magazines to ban unhealthy images of women were valuable and admirable, but the problem of male body image was unrepresented and disregarded. To criticise this under-representation of men is not a critique of feminism, but rather highlights the failure of men themselves to organise and lobby.

The 'inverse care law'

To understand the challenge of accessing treatment for men with body image disorders, it pays to consider the process by which we seek medical help in the first place. It would seem pretty obvious that if you get ill, you seek the help of a doctor and they attempt to cure you. However, studies suggest it is far more complicated than that, and the 'inverse care law' embodies that complexity.

A study by Wadsworth and others (1971) examined 'symptoms of disease' among 1000 people living in London. Out of these, only 49 were without any symptoms of illness; 562 had symptoms of disease, but dealt with those symptoms through means other than seeing a doctor. Only 168 people actually saw their GP, of whom 28 were referred to a specialist and only five ended up in hospital.

You can see that there is far more to having a symptom of illness than meets the eye. Three issues are particularly relevant to men with body image disorders. First, there is the problem of 'self-deception'. If you have been brought up to employ a 'stiff upper lip', you are less likely to seek help. Men with eating problems will often suffer in silence.

Second, there is the interpretation of the symptom. If you experience distressing symptoms but do not accept them as indicating an illness, then you will not seek help. This particularly applies in eating disorders and body image problems where men may not see behaviours such as weight loss or over-exercise as problematic at all.

Third, we have the 'inverse care law'. Even if you consider yourself to be ill, not everyone has equal access to health care. Bizarrely, the 'inverse care law' in the UK indicates that health care is less available in areas where it is

most needed. The poor, the disenfranchised and men have all been identified as most in need of health care but least able to access it.

Think about prominent UK health campaigns in the last few years.
Diseases affecting affluent and powerful women receive far more attention,
scrutiny and funding than men's health. Breast cancer charities thrive,
whilst prostate cancer fails to excite media or government interest. This is
not to criticise or begrudge the success of such charities, but to learn from
them. In the UK, charities such as Men's Health Forum, the UK's leading
charity working to improve men's health, and magazines such as *Men's
Health* have begun to redress the balance. Beat, the UK eating disorder
association, has begun to pay admirable attention to the specific problem of
body image issues in young men, and some proceeds from *The Invisible
Man* are donated to the Beat. But men's health, and body image problems
in particular, need to be considered in the context of a much broader
problem with men in our society.

Men in trouble?

Men are in trouble. The mere possession of the Y chromosome means you
are more likely to be in the lowest class in school. You are more likely to be
sent to jail. You are more likely to inject heroin. You are more likely to
be dependent on alcohol. You are more likely to kill yourself. You are less
likely to graduate from higher education. You are far more likely to lose
your job. Actuarially, women's employment rises and men's falls. Finally, if
you are lucky enough to have a job, you are more likely to have to work to
a ripe old age but then die far younger.

Feminists respond with 'So what?' The role of the man as a provider is
dead and buried. The role of man as a 'father' may be going the same way.
Freudian concepts of 'penis envy', or what Sylvia Plath dismissed as 'old
turkey neck and gizzards', seem redundant. Without rhetoric, Germaine
Greer wrote: 'I don't care much about phallic insecurity. Men created the
dream of the phallic. Women are perfectly happy with all the other stuff,
social status, power, intelligence.' Anthony Clare asked: 'Do we need men?
Do we need fathers? And if we do, what kind of men, what kind of fathers
do we need?' But the problems of men are not confined to men. They
impact on society in general, on our economy and the state of the nation.

In such a situation, it is not surprising that men with eating disorders are
more likely than women to fail to recognise their illness. They are more
likely than women to be underdiagnosed by their general practitioner (GP).
They are more likely than women to be given inadequate treatment by the
health service. They are less likely than women to be referred for treatment.
Once receiving treatment, they can experience stigmatisation as the 'sole'
man on predominantly female units. Finally, because they are treated later,
and in a more severe state of illness, outcomes of such treatments are worse.

In 1998, I published a study in the *International Journal of Eating Disorders* of the problems of managing men with eating disorders with my colleagues, Professor Lacey and Dr Key. On the basis of our experiences, we argued that a minority of men with eating disorders, and particularly multi-impulsive bulimia nervosa, simply cannot be successfully treated in a treatment programme with a feminist perspective. The question remains as to where they should be treated, when there are no alternatives.

Playing snakes and ladders

Men with eating disorders and body image problems can feel peculiarly shamed by their illness. The misconception that 'only women get eating disorders' makes male sufferers confused. The easiest way to deal with confusion is to ignore it, to pretend that nothing is going on, and so anorexia nervosa, bulimia, binge eating or muscle dysmorphia may go unrecognised by the sufferer for many years.

Just like female patients, men with eating disorders and body image problems present to their family doctor with some ambiguity of intention. They may be seeking to convince themselves that there is nothing wrong. They may be concealing from themselves, and from health-care professionals, the fuller extent of their abnormal behaviours. Thus they may contribute to misdiagnosis.

But a bigger portion of misdiagnosis emanates from health-care professionals themselves, who may not always understand the manifestation of eating disorders in men. For example, it is more common for men with anorexia nervosa to focus on 'shape' rather than 'weight'. Doctors and nurses dredge up vague memories that anorexia nervosa is associated with a fear of normal body weight. But men with body image problems are less likely to express concern with their weight than women. Thus, when these men fail to manifest an obsession with body weight, but instead are more focused on muscle tone, it is easy for health-care professionals to decide the men do not suffer from anorexia nervosa.

Again, most health-care professionals have a notion that women with anorexia nervosa may have problems with their menstrual periods, and this provides a nice, clear-cut diagnostic question. Some doctors struggle to find an equivalent question for men with eating disorders, and asking about early morning erections or 'wet dreams' can seem more difficult than taking a menstrual history. This is not a criticism of health-care professionals. Many medical schools provide very little education about eating disorders whatsoever, and when it comes to men with eating disorders the curriculum is severely limited. Health-care professionals can only be as good as their training. Under the circumstances, it is unsurprising that a man with an eating disorder may be misdiagnosed with other conditions, such as depression or psychoses.

No wonder the journey from illness to health can feel like a game of snakes and ladders. You throw the dice, finally pluck up the courage to seek help and shoot up a ladder, only to find yourself back where you started down the back of a particularly vicious snake. But eventually most men with eating disorder and body image problems will win the game.

The plight of men

Research by Beat

Beat, the UK eating disorders association, has always been ahead of its time, and in 2000 published *Eating Disorders in the United Kingdom: Review of the Provision of Health Care Services for Men with Eating Disorders*. First, they evaluated various clinics around the UK. They concluded that far fewer than 5 per cent of all referrals to specialist eating disorder clinics were represented by men, suggesting huge barriers to treatment. The Beat report highlighted some of the 'snakes' that you might encounter on your journey to recovery.

A lack of general knowledge and awareness 'in the community' was seen as one feature. For example, referrals of men with eating disorders would shoot right up after prominent television documentaries, and then decline when the issue was no longer in the media. Individual therapy (one-to-one help) seemed easier for men with eating disorders to accept than group treatment. Although not commented on in the report, one imagines that being the only man in a large group of women with eating disorders could be an isolating experience.

'Shame' was much more of an issue for men than women with eating disorders. Somehow men with eating disorders saw themselves as 'less' of a man, whilst the diagnosis was less of a threat to personal identity for woman. Cultural stereotypes of eating disorders provided a strong barrier to care. Health-care professionals were seen as construing a 'typical' eating disorder patient as middle-class girls, and anyone falling outside that false caricature risked misdiagnosis.

Where health-care professionals did diagnose men with eating disorders, generally it was at a much progressed stage in the development of the illness, typically involving severe malnutrition and therefore requiring intensive inpatient treatment. Men with eating disorders present later in their illness than women, and therefore can be harder to treat.

In the study of all specialist services in the UK, only one service was identified as providing gender specific treatment for men. All other services provided mixed treatments, with only a small minority of male patients. In the course of writing up their report, that single 'gender specific' service closed down. Not only were men with eating disorders likely to be treated within the much larger group of female patients, but the staff doing the treatment were predominantly female. Whilst some services regarded the inclusion of men in predominantly female psychotherapy groups as helpful, others saw this as a problem. Most men did not particularly regard the gender of their therapist as crucial. The men who were questioned were more concerned with the personal qualities of the therapist than their gender.

The Beat report went on to interview a number of men with eating disorders, and to tap into their personal experiences. Men from all over the country, and with a wide range of ages, were interviewed. All had struggled to accept the 'label' of the eating disorder as applied to a man. Excessive compulsive exercise was a common route into body image disparagement. Whilst a minority of the respondents were homosexual, particular pressures in the gay community were seen as a major factor in some cases. Most of the men were driven to seeking help by someone outside of themselves – a close friend or member of their family. In some instances it took the sufferer more than a decade to access help from a specialist service. In part, this was due to the time taken by the men themselves to acknowledge their problem, but stereotyping of eating disorders amongst health-care professionals was also a factor.

At times the level of ignorance in the Beat report was quite incredible. For example, one psychiatrist simply refused to accept that men ever developed bulimia nervosa. Many of the men were repeatedly investigated for physical causes of weight loss when a few pertinent psychological questions might have made the diagnosis in minutes. Even when admitting to an eating disorder, some of the men were simply not believed by health-care professionals – 'men don't get eating disorders'. Ability to access treatments seemed to depend on where you lived in the country. In the UK 50 per cent of the country has no specialist services whatsoever, and so there can exist a culture of ignorance that is particularly harmful for male patients. Where there is a 'specialist' eating disorder service, it is far more likely that the local medical students and student nurses who become the local family doctors and practice nurses will have had some awareness of body image problems.

The role of the family doctor seemed paramount. Many respondents had received excellent care from their family doctors who had been instrumental in acting as their 'advocate' in search of appropriate treatment. Despite examples of good practice, the Beat report represents an indictment of our approach to men with eating disorders. We would not accept this standard of care elsewhere in the health service.

Knowledge is power

What should you do? Knowledge is power, and there is no greater knowledge than self-knowledge. Simply by reading *The Invisible Man*, you are empowering yourself. You can begin to work out your own personal 'snakes' and 'ladders'. Try to make a list of them now. Perhaps your family doctor is particularly sympathetic and approachable (*ladder*) but the nearest eating disorder service is more than 80 miles away (*snake*)? Subsequent chapters of *The Invisible Man* will lead you through some of these issues. But the more you know about how the health system works, the easier it will be to navigate the health service.

In Chapter 18 I have written a 'consumer's guide' to seeking professional help. Beat in the UK and its equivalents elsewhere in the world, may make you feel less isolated and also can give practical advice on local specialist services. But in my opinion the best ladders and the worst snakes lie within you.

Chapter 2

Stories from the past

The first case of anorexia nervosa and Lord Byron's eating disorder

Through *The Invisible Man* I have tried to illustrate the issues by using modern stories. This narrative-based approach can convey a meaning that is lost in more scientific discussion. However, eating disorders are as old as the hills. The idea of them being 'modern conditions created by our media' is simplistic. Indeed, the first clinical descriptions date back to the seventeenth century.

The famous physician Richard Morton wrote *Phthisiologia: Or, a Treatise of Consumptions* in 1694. One of the two cases described by Richard Morton was of a young man. Men with eating disorders have thereafter consistently appeared within historical descriptions, and one of the more famous examples is Lord Byron. More contemporaneous examples abound, but comments on 'living' examples are intrusive and immoral. This chapter therefore seeks to explore two stories of men with eating disorders from the past.

'It flatters and deceives' – the first case of anorexia nervosa

Richard Morton was known as one of the foremost physicians in the seventeenth century. His clinical descriptions remain accurate today. Like all good academic doctors, he employed sharp powers of clinical observation to discern and describe a range of medical conditions, one of which we now know as anorexia nervosa. He described a condition of wasting of the body:

> Without any remarkable fever, cough or shortness of breath, in association with a bad digestion, upon which there follows a languishing weakness of nature, and a falling away of the flesh every day more and more.
>
> (p. 5)

He noted that in sufferers:

The face is pale . . . the stomach loathes everything but liquids, the strengths of the patient decline at that rate, that before fleshy parts of the body are evidently consumed, he is rendered plainly feeble, and almost always confined to his bed.

(p. 5)

He goes on to speculate about the causes of this strange condition:

The immediate cause of this distemper I apprehend to be in the system of the nerves proceeding from a preternatural state of the animal spirits and the destruction of the tone of the nerves . . . the causes which dispose the patient to this disease, I have for the most part observed to be violent passions of the mind . . . this distemper, as most other nervous diseases is chronicle but very hard to be cured, unless a physician be called at the beginning of it.

At first it flatters and deceives the patient, for which reason it happens for the most part that the physician is consulted too late.

(p. 5)

He then describes two cases, the second of which was a young man:

The son of the Very Reverend Minister Mr Steele . . . about the sixteenth year of his age, fell gradually into a total want of appetite, occasioned by his studying too hard, and the passions of his mind, and upon that into a universal atrophy, pining away more and more for the space of two years . . . and therefore I judged this consumption to be nervous, and to have its seat in the whole habit of the body, and to arise from the system of the nerves being distempered. . . .

I advised him to abandon his studies, to go into the country air, and to use riding, and a milk diet for a long time. By the use of which he recovered his health in a great measure, although he is not yet perfectly freed from a consumptive state.

(p. 10)

From this we observe an early recognition of the impact of emotion on appetitive function, ambivalence of seeking treatment, and most pertinently, the risk to men as well as women. The idea of the eating disorder 'flattering and deceiving' really gets to the heart of anorexia nervosa. That men should so evidently be recognised as suffering eating disorders in the seventeenth century, and yet become the 'invisible men' of the twenty-first century shows the power of dogma and stigma.

'Be warm, but pure; be amorous, but be chaste'

Fast forward by over one hundred years, and we come to the genius of Lord Byron. Byron epitomised romantic notions of inspired genius, rising above the tumult of his personal life to write the poem *Don Juan*, which provides a commentary on conflict between hunger and desire, strongly reflecting Byron's own lifelong war against his appetites.

Byron's family was notorious. His grandfather was seen as lecherous and amoral, bestowing similar traits on Byron's father, 'Mad Jack'. Mad Jack pursued an incestuous affair with his own sister, abandoning Byron's mother to poverty. Byron's mother grappled with depression, and came from a family of melancholics with a strong history of suicide.

Byron himself was physically and sexually abused at the hands of a nursemaid and in his teenage years was described as shy, melancholic and overweight. Combined with a clubfoot, his preoccupation with perceived physical imperfections caused him to manipulate his body shape by dietary restraint and excessive exercise. In adult life he was absorbed by his body image, describing himself as 'as vain of my curls as a girl of sixteen'. But this fragile and unsustainable state began to disintegrate into an eating disorder as recounted in *Byron's Letters and Journals*:

> I am grown very thin. . . . I have lost 18 pounds in my weight since January. I have taken every means to accomplish the end, by violent exercise and fasting, as I found myself too plump. I shall continue my exertions having no other amusement. I wear seven waistcoats and a great coat, run and play at cricket in this dress, till quite exhausted by excessive perspiration, use the hot bath daily, eat only a quarter pound of butcher's meat in twenty four hours, no suppers, or breakfast, only one meal a day.
>
> (p. 1128)

Later he goes on to note with pride: 'My ribs display skin of no great thickness, and my clothes have been taken in nearly half a yard.' In his diaries he gives an eloquent description of the drive from a relatively normal weight down to yet lower and lower skeletal body shape:

> I grow thin daily; since the commencement of my system I have lost 23 pounds in my weight. . . . I shall proceed and then stop, at least if I am not too fat, but shall always live temperately and take much exercise.
>
> I shall reduce myself to eleven, and there stop. . . . many of my acquaintance have hardly believed their optics, my visage is lengthened, I appear taller and somewhat slim and mirabile dictu, my hair once black and very dark brown is turned to a light chestnut, nearly approaching yellow, so that I am metamorphosed not a little.
>
> (p. 1434)

As his weight loss rapidly spiralled out of control he became a:

> leguminous eating [vegetable eating] aesthetic . . . my meal is generally
> at ye Alfred [a pub] where I munch my vegetables in place. . . . For a
> long time I have been restricted to an entire vegetable diet, neither fish
> or flesh coming within my regimen, so I expect a powerful stock of
> potatoes, greens and biscuit. . . . I am as thin as a skeleton – thinner
> than when you saw me at my first arrival in Venice and thinner than
> yourself.
>
> (p. 1436)

His extreme dieting was unsustainable and he graduated into a cyclical
pattern of bingeing and vomiting. His sister referred to this as: 'You know
his way is to fast until he is famished and then devour more than his
stomach in that weak state can bear – and so on' (Elwin 1962: 326).
 Lord Byron himself explained: 'When I do dine I gorge like . . . a boa
snake on fish and vegetables . . . not having tasted food for the preceding
forty-eight hours. I wish I could leave off eating altogether.' He was driven
to vegetarianism by a belief that consuming 'animal food engenders the
appetite of the animal fed upon'. This formed part and parcel of his own
personal battle against his sexual and emotional appetites, memorably
described as 'the wear and tear of the vulture passions'.

So the chaos of his internal world collided with the reality of the external
world, and Lady Caroline Lamb memorably described him as 'mad, bad
and dangerous to know'. Byron's life was a struggle between extremes, self-
denial versus hedonism, creativity versus chaos, anorexia nervosa versus
bulimia. His nervous impulses gave rise to considerable creativity, but he
found the restraint too much to handle, and moved into a condition of
obesity and alcohol misuse. Whilst assisting the Greeks in a rebellion
against Turkey, he suffered a stroke as a result of his excessive drinking,
chaotic eating habits and 'bleeding' performed at the hands of physicians
trying to temper his appetite. Shortly afterwards he died of a fever at the
age of 37, and was refused burial in Westminster Abbey. The conflict in his
nature seemed to mirror the conflict in the relationship between his mother
and his father, and this irreconcilable tension is summed up by his own
words:

> Be warm, but pure; be amorous, but be chaste.
> (*English Bards and Scotch Reviewers* 1809, l. 306)

Part II

Do you have a body image disorder?

Eating disorders and body image problems develop slowly and subtly. Very many men experience distress due to body image or disordered eating, and it is quite common to pass through a period in your life when emotional factors will influence your relationship with food and your body. This can become a more serious problem when the behaviours become ingrained habits, or when the thoughts preoccupy your mind. Once you start to use eating habits and exercise as a means of dealing with distressing emotions, then you might have a problem. The trouble is, it won't feel like a problem, it will feel like a solution to a problem. In the early stages of an eating disorder or body image problem, the pattern of behaviour can be experienced rather positively, much as the early stages of an alcoholic's drinking history may seem rather hedonistic. Sometimes, it is hard to decide if you have an eating disorder or not by yourself. You may need to confide in family or friends, or consult with a health-care professional. Many men with eating disorders are overwhelmed with feelings of shame and failure, and this can make it hard to take someone into your confidence.

The following is a guide to the diagnosis of anorexia nervosa, bulimia nervosa, muscle dysmorphia and obesity. It is not definitive. Some people show some but not all of the features which I am about to describe. For example, diagnosing anorexia nervosa involves a quantification of weight. Because men retain a degree of muscle bulk in the early stages of weight loss, many may not quite fulfil the diagnostic criteria for weight loss technically needed to make a diagnosis of anorexia nervosa. However, they may be as distressed, disabled and disempowered as another person with greater weight loss.

This has led many experts in the field of eating disorders to be dissatisfied with the current way of classifying and diagnosing eating disorders and related body image problems. A man may move from anorexia nervosa to bulimia nervosa and back again. A boy may be more disabled by a so-called atypical eating disorder than someone with a fully fledged illness. These atypical cases are at least as common as 'full' anorexia nervosa or bulimia. Therefore do not approach the following chapter as a definitive checklist, but rather see it as a guide.

Many health-care professionals struggle to make an accurate diagnosis of an eating disorder or muscle dysmorphia. It is therefore no wonder that sufferers can find it hard to place themselves on the spectrum between normal eating behaviour and abnormal. With this in mind, we developed a new technology for the screening of eating disorders using a simple memorable screening instrument, the SCOFF questionnaire. This has been widely validated on several different groups of people, including men with eating disorders. We know it detects many cases of anorexia nervosa and bulimia, though it is not applicable in the diagnosis of muscle dysmorphia. First, we established its validity in people with eating disorders at one of the UK's largest eating disorder units at St George's hospital, London. Second, we looked at its use in students. Third, we examined its potential in a large group of people attending their GP (family doctor). We found it detected most cases of anorexia and bulimia. However, it also scored positive for some people who did not have an eating disorder. Some of these may have had past disordered eating, but some may simply have had other explanations for scoring 'positive'. Whilst the SCOFF questionnaire has been widely adapted throughout the UK and elsewhere in the world as a 'rough and ready' means of raising the index of suspicion that someone may have an eating disorder, it is not 'diagnostic'. In other words, it is a preliminary, but is insufficient in itself.

The SCOFF questions

A score of two or more positives indicates the possibility of anorexia nervosa or bulimia.

- **S**   Do you make yourself sick because you feel uncomfortably full?
- **C**   Do you worry that you have lost control over what you eat?
- **O**   Have you recently lost more than one stone (14 lbs) in a three-month period?
- **F**   Do you believe yourself to be fat when others say you are thin?
- **F**   Would you say that food dominates your life?

In my opinion, eating disorders and muscle dysmorphia, are ultimately representative of states of mind, and cannot be reduced to simple checklists of this kind. However, checklists do have value in focusing the mind, so it is unsurprising that our questionnaire has proved popular. To make a judgement on whether you really have an eating disorder or muscle dysmorphia requires far more rigorous and detailed evaluation, and the following narrative is designed to give you guidance.

Chapter 3

Anorexia nervosa

Diagnosis

Anorexia nervosa can be defined along three different levels. First, there is the way you think (psychopathology). Second, there is your behaviour. Third, there is the physical consequence. The diagnosis of anorexia nervosa is on the basis shown in Box 3.1.

Box 3.1 Anorexia nervosa

1 A body weight less than 85 per cent of that expected for one's age and height. For example, in an adult this might involve weight loss, or in a child this might involve failure of weight gain during growth. Body mass index (BMI) is a rough and ready indicator of this, though it has many flaws, as described.

2 Absolute terror of gaining weight, though already underweight.

3 Distortion of body image, for example, with either an excessive influence of body shape on self-esteem, or denial of severity of low body weight.

4 In men, evidence of hormonal changes such as reduction in testosterone.

We usually think of two different subtypes of anorexia nervosa. The *purging/ bingeing type* involves additional regular episodes of binge eating or purging behaviours such as self-induced vomiting, misuse of laxatives, diuretics or enema. The *restricting type* is defined by the absence of these regular behaviours.

Some men may have some, but not all, of these features. For example, despite significant weight loss, their current weight may not be quite as low as that specified in Box 3.1. Technically this is diagnosed as the clumsily titled eating disorder not otherwise specified, of which Chapter 4 gives further descriptions. The diagnosis of anorexia nervosa sounds rather full of medical jargon, but it essentially involves low weight, fear of weight gain, distortion of body image, behaviours relating to weight loss and physical consequences of these factors.

Low weight

Someone with anorexia nervosa maintains a weight abnormally low for their age and height. For an adult this may involve weight loss. For a teenager this may simply involve a failure to make the expected weight gain. Someone with anorexia nervosa is typically at least 15 per cent lower than the weight expected for their weight and height. An easier estimate of weight applies a formula known as the body mass index (BMI). This can be useful for adults, but less so for children and teenagers. It is a rather rough-and-ready approach. Some famously fit boxers would be regarded as overweight using BMI alone, as it fails to account for muscle bulk.

The body mass index (BMI) is calculated by taking your weight in kilograms and dividing it by your height in metres squared. For example, if you weigh 60 kg and your height is 1.7 metres, your BMI would be:

$$60 \ / \ (1.7 \times 1.7) = 20.8 \ \text{kg/m}^2$$

An indication of healthy weight for adults is given by the BMI range of 20 to 25. We diagnose anorexia nervosa in men with BMIs less than 17.5 and significant overweight at BMIs higher than 27. However, I have treated many men with anorexia nervosa who have fluctuated between low (less than 17.5) and low–normal (18–20). There can often be little to distinguish the two in terms of distress and disability. People with eating disorders are rightly irritated by being defined only in terms of their BMI. Rather like the SCOFF questionnaire, BMI gives us an indication of a problem, but not a comprehensive description.

Fear of weight gain

The second diagnostic criterion is the intense fear of gaining weight or of becoming fat, despite being underweight. Many men show a fear of weight gain, but in anorexia nervosa it is taken to the nth degree. A further discussion of this is provided below.

Distortion of body image

Third, there is a disturbance in the experience of your body weight and shape, with an evaluation of yourself largely based on these factors, and sometimes a denial of the severity of low body weight. This is one aspect of diagnosis that does not fully do justice to men with eating disorders. Many men with eating disorders are not particularly concerned over issues of body weight. They are less likely than women to examine or define themselves in terms of weighing scales. They are far more likely to show a preoccupation with the shape of their body. When health-care professionals are trying to diagnose eating disorders, they often look for signs of distress and emotion concerning weight. Yet some men with anorexia nervosa will quite happily allow themselves to be weighed, and show a degree of indifference to the results. Their greater concern focuses on their physical appearance, and particular parts of the body such as stomach, buttocks, legs, chest or face.

Thus many men with anorexia nervosa will be showing a quite marked distortion of how they perceive these body areas. By distortion I don't just mean a visual distortion. It is also the value placed on the bodily parts. There is a sense of having less value as a man if you fail to conform to an impossible body image ideal.

Behaviours relating to weight loss

We look for particular patterns of eating behaviour and calorie burning. Weight loss is self-induced by the avoidance of fattening foods. Very many men with anorexia nervosa will also be utilising excessive exercise as a means of weight manipulation. For some men, they are driven to be better athletes, and certain sportsmen are at particular risk of developing anorexia nervosa. These include boxers, runners, gymnasts and wrestlers. Sometimes, the excessive exercise is a reaction to having been slightly overweight as a child. More often it is driven by complex emotional factors, allowing control over difficult emotions. It may be compulsive. Chapter 8 deals with exercise abuse in greater detail.

Men with anorexia nervosa may also use a range of other behaviours to manipulate their weight. These include self-induced vomiting, using laxatives to control weight, taking appetite suppressants and slimming pills or water tablets (diuretics). Some men who abuse stimulant drugs such as cocaine and amphetamines may actually be doing so in order to maintain a low body mass, rather than out of hedonism.

Physical consequences

Finally, in the diagnosis of anorexia in men we look for hormonal consequences. Men with anorexia nervosa often experience a reduction in testosterone levels, which may create a loss of sexual interest or even impotence. Likewise, on recovery from anorexia nervosa there will often be a resumption of sexual interest, including the experience of wet dreams or a greater frequency of masturbation.

Particularly where the anorexia nervosa has begun before or during puberty, there may be evidence of delayed growth, in terms of height or even the genitals. A preoccupation with genital size is not uncommon in some men with anorexia nervosa, but obviously can be very embarrassing to discuss openly.

What if anorexia nervosa and bulimia overlap?

We distinguish a *restrictive* type of anorexia nervosa from a bulimic or *binge eating/purging type*. In restrictive anorexia nervosa the man with anorexia nervosa will typically be starving himself or over-exercising. In the binge eating or purging subtype there may be evidence of episodic overeating, or purging using vomiting, laxative misuse, diuretics or enemas.

Anorexia nervosa trumps bulimia nervosa, because it tends to be even more serious, to have more complications and to be harder to treat. Therefore we talk of a bulimic subtype of anorexia nervosa rather than anorectic subtype of bulimia nervosa. Men with the bulimic subtype of anorexia nervosa can find it a bit harder to recover, as they have to grapple with two different sets of behaviour, and are more likely to use a repertoire of other maladaptive behaviours such as alcohol and drug misuse.

The anorectic state-of-mind

Abnormal thinking is the essence of anorexia nervosa. Judging someone in terms of their weight or behaviour can be useful at times, but it is the state of mind that defines the condition. This really represents the core of the disorder. Tapping into the state of mind of the anorectic is necessary both to diagnosis and to treatment. We can separate the state of mind of anorexia nervosa into core and non-core features.

The core feature of anorexia nervosa is an absolute dread of normal body shape and weight. There is a preoccupation with schemes to lose weight or to modify body shape. The fear of weight gain becomes an absolute terror. Eventually self-esteem becomes solely based on what your body looks like, and not on all the other factors of a good life. Accessing and assessing this distortion of thinking is essential to diagnosis. However, it can be extremely difficult. While it can be very distressing for the person with anorexia nervosa, the alternative may be even more distressing. In simple terms, having anorexia nervosa is bad, but not having it is even worse.

The psychological conflicts that give rise to anorexia nervosa are temporarily resolved by anorexia nervosa. That is why a man with anorexia nervosa will rarely admit to having a problem in the early stages. Many people are in denial, and instead may present the physical complications. One complex aspect of anorexia nervosa is the issue of *appetite*. The word anorexia is used in medicine to mean *loss of appetite*. However, most people with anorexia nervosa have a normal appetite that they are subverting. Weight loss through loss of appetite is common in conditions such as depression as well as a range of physical disorders. In the early stages of anorexia nervosa appetite tends to be quite normal, though of course after a while one's sense of hunger becomes distorted by prolonged starvation.

The starving mind

Many of the mental features of anorexia nervosa, which we experience, are partly explained by the physical state of starvation. We know this through a range of studies, and so think of these as non-core features. This is not to say that they aren't important.

First, we have examined the short-term effects of calorific deprivation in laboratory studies. Second, we have examined the effects of malnutrition on emotion and behaviour in larger groups of people who have experienced malnutrition. Even in the absence of anorexia nervosa, it is common to see the following features in people who are emaciated and have a 'starving mind'. Characteristically there is depression and irritability. When deprived of food, people become socially withdrawn, keeping themselves to themselves. The biological impact of starvation reduces sexual libido and it can also affect one's ability to pay attention or to concentrate. Some men who are experiencing starvation will develop a range of obsessional ruminations and rituals. They may hoard possessions, including food, repetitively count those possessions or lay them out in a strictly ordered line.

Depression is a very common feature of the starving mind. Of course, for an important minority of men with anorexia nervosa depression comes first, and may require vigorous treatment of itself. However, many more men with anorexia nervosa and depression are better treated by nutritional rehabilitation than antidepressant medication, the depression tending to improve as nutrition also improves.

Some men who develop anorexia nervosa have always been introverted, or have lacked self-esteem. However, others become increasingly socially withdrawn due to the starving mind, as well as the wish to conceal their illness from others. Often other changes in personality are quite inconsistent with how you were before the illness developed. A previously 'perfect boy' may become angry, argumentative, aggressive and even deceitful. This becomes quite complex for family and friends. Who is to blame? Blaming the illness rather than the person can be an important step forward in improving relationships with family and friends.

Initially, the starving mind is just a small part of your personality. But gradually it takes over until it can become your main source of identity in a fragile ego. It may give you a sense of control over aspects of yourself, including your feelings, thoughts and sometimes sexuality. Where you have major problems in relationships with other people, the anorexia nervosa initially appears to resolve these problems by making you indifferent to them. Of course, this is a fool's paradise, as this never lasts for long. But the evil fact about anorexia nervosa is that it can initially appear to be your good friend, and too late you realise that it is your enemy.

Behaviour

The most obvious behaviour in anorexia nervosa is extreme calorific restriction. Sometimes the pattern of this will mirror various dietary fads that are seen throughout the media, and these may change with time. For example, whilst very many men with anorexia nervosa may be genuine vegans and vegetarians and maintaining a consistent ethical stance, some may use extreme veganism to conceal their eating disorder. Similarly, some men with anorexia nervosa do suffer from very genuine food allergies, but we have seen a rise in people professing food allergies which are later unsubstantiated by physical tests.

As well as simply eating a calorifically restricted diet, there are often odd habits around mealtimes. Some men with anorexia nervosa will secretly dispose of their food, or develop rituals. These might include cutting food into small portions, eating very slowly or using peculiar utensils to eat food. They may eat at unusual times of the day; for example, starving throughout the daytime and eating only at night. It is very common for men with anorexia nervosa to avoid or refuse to eat in the company of other people. Either to conceal weight loss from others, or to reduce the hunger pangs, some men will consume excessive quantities of fluid such as water or fizzy drinks. Excessive consumption of fluids produces its own range of medical complications.

Exercise

Excessive exercise is particularly common in men with anorexia nervosa. Chapter 8 tackles the issue in greater detail. Initially this is conscious exercise, usually solitary in nature and sometimes representing a 'pay-off'. For example: 'I had no choice but to eat dinner with my family, but I will get rid of it later by doing 200 press-ups.' Initially conscious overactivity can later become unconscious, and be another manifestation of the starving mind. We believe that some of this may represent a sort of 'primitive foraging behaviour', linked to a distressing sense of restlessness and often insomnia.

Purging

Some men with anorexia nervosa will use purging as a means of modifying their weight. Purging behaviour in anorexia nervosa has been described as the 'ominous variant' by Professor Gerald Russell, and can be particularly threatening to physical well-being. Purging behaviours include self-induced vomiting, laxative misuse, consumption of specific purgatives, use of enemas and diuretics, taking slimming pills or stimulant drugs for weight manipulation purposes.

Physical complications

Anorexia nervosa involves a state of mind as well as behaviours. But we also need to consider the physical consequences. A proper understanding of physical complications really requires a proper medical examination, and so the following should be seen only as a 'rough guide'.

Fatigue

Fatigue is a common physical presentation of anorexia nervosa in men. A lack of nutrition makes you tired and weary, and the psychological battle adds to this. Disturbed sleep makes it ten times worse. Sleep is a complex phenomenon. Many people think of sleep purely in terms of quantity, but quality is more important. Sleep occurs in a series of phases, of which you may be most familiar with 'rapid eye movement' (REM) sleep when dreams are most prominent. Anorexia nervosa disrupts the architecture of sleep profoundly, not only reducing its quantity but also its quality. Sleep becomes less restorative or healing, and many men with anorexia nervosa fail to wake refreshed.

Cardiovascular system

Anorexia nervosa affects the heart and cardiovascular system. When your doctor has diagnosed anorexia nervosa, they would normally conduct a thorough examination of the cardiovascular system. It is not uncommon for men with anorexia nervosa to have a slow pulse rate. Whilst we often associate a slow pulse with physical fitness, it can also be problematic. Coupled with a low blood pressure, men with anorexia nervosa may therefore experience dizzy spells, particularly when rising from a sitting position. Some may even experience faints or 'funny turns'. Because your heart is no longer pumping efficiently, you may experience sensitivity to the cold. Hands and feet appear mottled and blue, known as Acrocyanosis, sometimes with thinning of the skin. In extreme case, people with anorexia nervosa can suffer hypothermia.

Hormones

As we have already discussed, anorexia nervosa has a big impact on male hormones, with a reduction in levels of testosterone. This can create sexual problems, including loss of sexual libido and occasionally impotence. Infertility is common at low weight. Where you are not in a regular relationship, this may be less apparent. Instead, you may notice that you have less sexual interest or that you are no longer having early morning erections. The good news is that these problems resolve when you 'get better'. You can put the physical complications right.

Gut

Anorexia nervosa has many effects on the gut. The most common experiences are symptoms in your tummy. You may find yourself constipated, or feeling excessively full after relatively small amounts of food. Sometimes, you might be fearful that your stomach is actually going to 'burst'. Most often, this is because your brain has lost touch with your stomach. Relatively small amounts of food give an erroneous message to the brain that you are completely full. You can no longer trust your head to tell you if you're full or hungry.

Teeth

For men who are using purging behaviours, there may be problems in the mouth and throat. Dental problems are not uncommon, and these can be made worse by the tendency to avoid seeing the dentist in the first place. Further details on the physical effects of purging are given in the next chapter.

Skin

Several years ago we published a study looking at the skins of people with anorexia nervosa. We found that it was common to experience an unpleasant itchy sensation, particularly at low weight, and this tended to get better as you gained weight. Thus, skin problems are quite common in men with anorexia. Another consequence of prolonged low weight is the production of 'downy hair' known as 'Lanugo hair'. This hair growth is seen in premature babies and, although poorly understood, is thought to be a primitive response against the risk of hypothermia. Such hair growth is inconsequential in itself, but can make body image problems much worse.

Bones

One of the most serious effects of anorexia nervosa on the body can be least evident. Chronic anorexia nervosa is associated with a loss of bone density, which can lead into osteoporosis. Osteoporosis is a condition we normally associate with postmenopausal women, and it can give rise to brittle bones, with a serious risk of fractures. For doctors treating anorexia nervosa, it is usually routine to carry out a bone scan in order to determine severity of osteoporosis. This is extremely difficult to determine by other means. The best treatment of osteoporosis in anorexia nervosa is weight gain, and conventional treatments of osteoporosis don't seem to be very effective in anorexia nervosa. The impact of osteoporosis can be devastating.

There is a wide variety of physical consequences of anorexia nervosa, and the above is a simple guide to those which you are most likely to be aware of. Doctors managing anorexia nervosa would carry out a comprehensive physical examination, a variety of blood tests and sometimes an evaluation of your heart using the electrocardiogram (ECG).

It is important to note that most of the physical complications of anorexia nervosa can be reversed with adequate weight gain, but equally most cannot be addressed without that weight gain. Thus, when you are trying to make a cost-benefit analysis of remaining unwell or getting better, understanding some of these physical complications can be critical.

Conclusions

Anorexia nervosa is a complex amalgam of psychological, behavioural and physical features. Some people have some, but not all, of those features. The judgement as to whether or not you have anorexia nervosa is quite a complex one, and may require the subtle evaluation of an outsider. Because some of the symptoms of anorexia nervosa are experienced as slightly gratifying in the early stages, it can be very difficult to make a judgement about yourself, as you will have a tendency to deny or minimise your symptoms. For men with anorexia nervosa in particular, this book would strongly recommend seeking professional help (see the 'consumer's guide' in Chapter 8).

Chapter 4

Bulimia nervosa and binge eating

Bulimia nervosa

The diagnosis of anorexia nervosa is tethered to clear parameters such as weight and health-care professionals are more adept at diagnosing it. On the other hand, bulimia can be harder to spot, and studies suggest that most cases are never properly diagnosed or treated. Typically, men with bulimia nervosa have a normal or slightly above normal weight, even though that weight may fluctuate markedly. Some men with binge eating problems will have developed significant overweight. Words like bingeing can feel hard to define, and the essence of bulimia nervosa is the emotional motivation behind the overeating. This becomes a subject of judgement.

The 'formal' diagnosis of bulimia nervosa is made according to the criteria shown in Box 4.1.

Box 4.1 Bulimia nervosa

1 Episodes of binge eating that are recurrent, and involve eating a large amount of food rapidly (e.g. within any two-hour period). There is a feeling of loss of control during the episode.

2 Compensatory behaviours to prevent weight gain, such as self-induced vomiting; fasting, misuse of laxatives, diuretics, enemas, or other medications, or excessive exercise.

3 Bingeing and compensation both occur, on average, **at least twice a week for three months**.

4 Self-evaluation is excessively based on body shape and weight.

5 This definition of bulimia nervosa also permits two subtypes:
   - *purging type*: in which there is self-induced vomiting or misuse of laxatives, diuretics or enemas
   - *non-purging type* in which there are other compensatory behaviours, such as fasting or excessive exercise, but not self-induced vomiting or the misuse of laxatives, diuretics or enemas.

Crucial to the diagnosis is a pattern of *binge eating* and subsequent *compensatory behaviours*, coupled to *body image disturbance*.

Binge eating disorder

Binge eating can occur in the absence of these compensatory behaviours, and a formal diagnosis of binge eating disorder is made according to the criteria shown in Box 4.2.

Box 4.2 Binge eating disorder

1 Episodes of binge eating that are recurrent, and involve eating a large amount of food rapidly (e.g. within any two-hour period). There is a feeling of loss of control during the episode.
2 There is a strong emotional component to the binge eating.
3 The binge eating occurs, on average, at least two days a week for six months.
4 The binge eating is not associated with regular compensatory behaviours (e.g. purging, fasting, excessive exercise).

Of course, very many people show some, but not all, of these features. We used to call these cases 'subclinical', but evidence suggests that men with so-called subclinical eating disorders may be suffering just as much distress and disability as men with 'full' conditions. Scientists therefore resort to the clumsily titled eating disorders not otherwise specified as a rag-bag of assorted diagnoses:

Eating disorders not otherwise specified

These are disorders of eating that do not meet the criteria for any specific eating disorders in the six categories, as shown in Box 4.3.

Box 4.3 Eating disorders not otherwise specified

1 All the features of anorexia nervosa, without evidence of hormonal disturbance (in women, regular periods).
2 All the features of anorexia nervosa except, despite significant weight loss, current weight in the normal range.
3 All the features of bulimia nervosa except a lesser frequency of binge eating and compensatory mechanisms.

4   Regular use of compensatory behaviours, but in the absence of binge eating (e.g. self-induced vomiting after eating small amounts of food).

5   Repeated chewing and spitting out, but not swallowing large amounts of food.

6   Binge eating disorder: as described above.

Many men will occasionally binge eat without necessarily having a fully fledged eating disorder. So when does transient 'emotional eating' become entrenched bulimia nervosa or binge eating? It can be easier to consider these issues by looking at an individual's experience than the jargon-heavy language above.

When I was fifteen I began to really hate my body. I moved into a new class at school, and people used to tease me and call me 'moon face'. I went on a diet but I didn't really know what I was doing. I would try to eat nothing but fruit all day long, but in the evenings I just couldn't keep it up and I began to binge eat on crisps and chocolate. I would just eat and eat until I couldn't eat anything more. I felt I was going to burst.

Every time I binged I felt disgusted at myself, but that just made me want to do it even more. Although I wanted to lose weight I actually began to gain.

I remember reading an article about making yourself sick, and I tried it for myself. The first time I did it, it was amazing. I suddenly thought, 'Here's a way of letting myself binge whenever I want, but I don't need to pay the price.'

Eventually I wasn't eating any regular meals at all, but simply starving myself during the day and then bingeing and vomiting in the evenings. That's when it really took hold of me.

Such descriptions clearly convey *emotional* qualities of binge eating, *body image disparagement* and *habitual nature* of behaviours. Anorexia nervosa and bulimia nervosa have a lot in common with each other, and some commentators have even suggested that they exist on a spectrum. It is certainly not uncommon for men with anorexia nervosa to move into a period of bulimia. Men with both conditions find themselves using their eating pattern to deal with difficult emotions and conflicts, much as alcoholics may use booze to quash their feelings. There is the same preoccupation with body shape and weight. Men with bulimia nervosa or binge eating are more likely to be preoccupied with shape than weight, in contrast with women. Body image can be a greater preoccupation than absolute body mass.

What do we mean by binge eating?

As you can see from the definitions above, there are three essential qualities to a 'binge'. First, a *large amount* of food is consumed, far more than would be regarded as normal by other people. Some men with eating disorders will feel intense guilt at any amount of food intake, hence they may wrongly talk of bingeing when in fact they are consuming relatively small amounts of food. Thus some men with anorexia nervosa will say they are bingeing when in fact they are consuming nothing more than a couple of dry crackers.

The second element of binge eating is the element of *time*. Some men consume large amounts of food by constantly grazing throughout the day. What we mean by a binge is the consumption of large amounts of food over a relatively short period of time, typically defined as less than two hours.

The third, and most definitive, component of binge eating is the *emotional motivation* behind it. Some people overeat out of hedonism, but there is nothing self-indulgent about bulimia nervosa or binge eating, and no pleasure derived from the experience. Binge eating is driven by a sense of loss of control and motivated by negative emotions. In the first few minutes there can be a sense of gratification, but very rapidly this is replaced with distress or 'dissociation'. Dissociation is a common feature in binge eating and means an almost trance-like state of detachment, in which feelings and thoughts and perceptions are experienced as detached from the rest of the self. Descriptions of dissociation are most commonly found in narratives of soldiers' responses to wartime stress. The early scenes of the film *Saving Private Ryan* convey that experience authentically. Bulimia nervosa and binge eating can feel like warfare. One man described his experiences of 'binge eating' as 'almost like I was watching someone else doing it'. So we refer to a binge when we mean consumption of a *large amount* of food *rapidly* with a sense of *loss of control*:

> I plan my binges in advance. I drive home via a particular supermarket and buy four or five big tubs of ice cream. I feel excitement, but not pleasure, at the idea of eating it all.
>
> As soon as I walk through the door I can't wait. I begin to eat the ice cream, sometimes even in the corridor. Immediately I start, I know I won't stop until it is all gone. By then I am not really thinking straight, I am just gulping it down, walking around my flat and sometimes leaving such a messy trail that I feel disgusted at myself.
>
> I just force it down myself as quickly as I can and I won't stop until either it's all gone or I can't get anything more into me. As soon as that happens, I sit there in a complete blank.

> Then the thoughts and feelings start to come back, and I feel disgusting and fat and horrible. Within less than a minute I will need to do something about it, so I go upstairs and use the back of my toothbrush to make myself sick. At first I wasn't very good a t making myself sick, but now it's almost like I have trained myself, and I will immediately vomit everything until there is nothing left.
>
> By then I don't feel just physically empty but emotionally empty. I don't feel sad or happy, I just feel nothing. It's not a 'nice' nothingness but there is something slightly 'calm' about it. Of course it doesn't last long, and as soon as that effect wears off I hate myself and want to hurt myself.

Men who binge will eat any combination of fats, protein or carbohydrates. The notion of bingeing as being a 'carbohydrate craving' simply isn't true. Some men will have particular binge foods that they associate with binge episodes. These may be biscuits or ice cream or chocolates or cakes, and very often they are the same foods that are forbidden during the day. They tend to be foods that have been invested in an emotional quality, and experienced as reward or punishment.

Sometimes binge eating occurs every day of the week, but it can be counterbalanced by 'restrained' days. Thus many men with bulimia nervosa will have 'anorectic' days of eating virtually nothing, and more 'bulimic' days of binge eating. There can be a clear pattern in the timing of binge eating. Some men will binge only in the evenings, or after a particularly difficult meeting in the afternoon. Some will binge mid-morning, having eaten nothing for the past 24 hours. Typically, binge eating is a private affair hidden from others, and a considerable amount of pre-planning may go into keeping it hidden.

Initially, there may be clear-cut emotions that precipitate episodes. Identifying emotional triggers is part of treatment. Some men binge in response to loneliness, or existential despair. Some men may be motivated by anger or self-disgust. Others have described an almost frenetic excitement in anticipation of binge eating. Examining the emotional causes and consequences of binge eating can form one important component of breaking the cycle.

As well as the 'trigger' emotions, there can sometimes be personal circumstances that have caused or exacerbated binge eating. Episodes of bulimia may be precipitated by major life events, such as moving home or experiencing bereavement. Interpersonal stress may be an important factor, and this is why a form of psychotherapy known as 'Interpersonal Therapy' is known to be effective in treating bulimia nervosa. Many men who experience binge eating or bulimia do so as a result of relationship problems:

> When I first started to binge I had just split up with my girlfriend. To make matters worse, she had begun seeing my brother. I felt I had lost two people and not just one.

Bingeing was always something I would do in the evenings, simply because it was so hard to binge during the working day. I kept a special cupboard, locked, where all my binge foods were stored. If ever that cupboard started to empty I would become really worried. They weren't even foods that I particularly like. But in some ways I was doing it because I hated myself, but I felt so lonely.

The thing about the binge eating was it worked. I did feel 'comfortably numb' and it made it easier just to sit there in that empty flat without having to think too much about how I felt, or how unhappy I was. As soon as I did it, I felt incredibly disgusted with myself. 'Disgusted' doesn't do it justice. I felt myself to be revolting and fat. I felt so horrible in myself that I didn't want to see anyone else, because I did not want to inflict myself on them.

What is the difference between binge eating and bulimia nervosa?

Some people binge on a regular basis, and develop a condition that has become known as binge eating disorder, as defined above. This implies regular cycles of binge eating at least three times a week over a period of at least six months. This extremely distressing condition results in weight gain, and a significant proportion of people who are overweight or even obese suffer from binge eating disorder.

Many people who binge eat will then respond to their binge with some behaviour designed to compensate. When this occurs at least twice a week over a three-month period we talk about the diagnosis of bulimia nervosa. Of course many people will do so to lesser or greater degrees, and to some extent these definitions are rather arbitrary. What counts is the emotional motivation behind the episodes.

'Compensation' for a binge may involve a wide variety of behaviours. It may involve making yourself vomit, taking laxatives, purgatives or enemas, using diuretics or slimming pills, taking stimulant drugs such as amphetamines or cocaine, over-exercising in order to burn calories, or simply extreme dieting. Self-induced vomiting is the most typical form of compensation in bulimia nervosa. Initially, vomiting is induced by mechanical means such as sticking fingers down the back of your throat or using an implement. However, later it can be a 'learned' reflex, requiring nothing but the thought to produce the action. There are many and varied means by which people with bulimia nervosa will induce vomiting, and to list them all may be counter-productive, so I will not do so.

In the initial stages of bulimia nervosa, many men describe the discovery of self-induced vomiting in positive terms. Episodes of bingeing are distressing, whereas vomiting is initially a relief of difficult emotion, a novel means of weight manipulation. However, the impact of vomiting is both physically and psychologically disastrous. Many people who simply binge during times of unhappiness will spontaneously get better when they feel happier in themselves, but the vomiting begins to perpetuate a vicious cycle. The pattern of bingeing and then vomiting becomes deeply ingrained, such that even when the difficult circumstances have resolved, the habit gets its claws in you.

Physically, you oscillate between states of extreme satiation and extreme starvation. Psychologically, you oscillate between extreme self-disgust and complete numbness. These vicious emotional and physiological cycles perpetuate the disorder. Although the vomiting may begin as a means of compensating for overeating, later vomiting becomes the cause of overeating as it perpetuates extreme starvation. The more you vomit, the more you binge. People have talked of this as a pattern of 'addiction', though in the opinion of many eating disorder experts the term addiction doesn't quite do it justice. Of course, vomiting is not just addictive within the limits of that term, it is also physically dangerous. People who regularly vomit will experience changes in blood salts that can affect the way the heart and brain work. Vomiting makes people feel exhausted and so, if there are difficult challenges in your life to be faced, it becomes that much harder to face them.

Some people who binge eat will then respond by extreme calorific restrictions. Many of the men I have treated with bulimia nervosa have set themselves very rigid 'rules'. You set yourself impossibly high standards, then beat yourself up when you fail to achieve those standards. Binge eating thus represents a breaking of rigid rules, and subsequent dieting is a form of punishment or resumption of control in its aftermath.

Some men will try to eat absolutely nothing whatsoever whilst others will plan unsustainably small amounts of calorific intake. Paradoxically, it is this sense of starvation that goes on to trigger the next binge eating episode. Thus, one of the most effective strategies in lessening the frequency of bulimia nervosa is actually to regularise and increase calorific intake. Bingeing and then starving is unsustainable at a physical level. Reducing the extremities of satiation and starvation inoculates you against the risks of bulimia.

People who binge will sometimes then attempt to 'empty themselves' by taking laxatives or slimming pills. In real terms, laxatives do absolutely nothing to calorific intake. They act on a part of the gut that has no bearing on calorific intake and is more involved in absorption of water. Thus, taking laxatives in response to binge eating is not only dangerous, it is also entirely ineffective. Most people who take laxatives are well aware of this fact, but they continue to do so because it makes them feel cleansed. It is the sense of being somehow purified which drives an otherwise dangerous behaviour. Chronic laxative misuse can have a profound impact on the body. Just as with vomiting, it can severely impact on essential blood salts. That is why it is so important for people with bulimia nervosa to have physical tests conducted by a suitably qualified health-care professional. In addition, chronic laxative misuse will affect the way your gut works. Many laxatives work by stimulating the gut muscle, but after a while the effect wears off, and you need more and more of the same laxative to have the equivalent effect. Eventually the gut becomes overwhelmed with this stimulation and may stop working. In mild cases this can result in constipation, but in more serious cases laxative misuse will permanently damage the gut and may require surgical interventions.

What causes bulimia nervosa and binge eating disorder?

Later in this book, I discuss the causes of eating disorders in greater detail. For bulimia we know there is genetic vulnerability. There is increasing evidence of a direct genetic link. This link is not only with eating disorders, but also with mood disorders such as depression and alcoholism, as well as personality and temperament. Genes for certain body shapes and sizes will run in families. The tendency to put on 'puppy fat', that most horrible of expressions, has a genetic element. Psychological responses to this can lead on to bulimia nervosa or binge eating.

We know that eating disorders run in families. As well as the direct genetic association, to a large extent this is due to the '*modelling*' of behaviour between parent/sibling and child. The boy who develops bulimia may be doing so at the unconscious invitation of their parent, or brother, or sister. This is not to blame families for causing bulimia, but to suggest that understanding family dynamics can sometimes be helpful.

The overlap between depression and bulimia is considerable. In some instances bulimia nervosa becomes the man's way of coping with depression, albeit temporarily and ineffectively. Bingeing dampens down the extreme emotions associated with depression.

Temperament plays a strong part in predisposing to the illness. The combination of chronically low self-esteem and yet striving for perfection creates the mindset of 'black-and-white thinking', in which if things aren't wonderful then they must be terrible. I have discussed above how the setting of impossibly high standards can sometimes set the bulimic man up to fail. Moving between a sense of triumph and a sense of disaster is common in the 'cognitive structure' of men who go on to develop bulimia nervosa.

In some instances low self-esteem is the result of difficult childhood experiences. In a significant minority of cases, there may have been a history of childhood sexual abuse or other traumatic experiences. There may have been emotional deprivation or major problems within the family during childhood. However, there can be a danger of exaggerating these issues, and it is worth reiterating that most men with bulimia nervosa have had happy, healthy childhoods. Seeking to explain everything because of some past trauma can be a dangerous game, but in some instances trauma can indeed be relevant. In particular, we know that the emotional experience of dissociation described above is strongly associated with traumatic experiences, and sometimes with post traumatic stress disorder.

The same cultural factors that predispose to anorexia nervosa are also relevant in bulimia nervosa. The impossible body image ideal to which young men are now exposed is quite incompatible with a sustainable and healthy life. Oscillating between extreme dieting and binge eating is the result of these impossible aspirations, and we have seen a genuine increase in the prevalence of bulimia nervosa amongst young men over the past eight years. Men are more likely to develop bulimia nervosa when they work in industries in which weight and appearance are pertinent. I have treated men with bulimia who have worked within the fashion industry, the media or other aspects of performing arts. Equally I have treated men for whom manipulation of weight is part of their job, including jockeys, boxers and athletes. Responsible holistic men's magazines have taken the issue of male eating disorders very seriously. All too often, however, bingeing and bulimia nervosa in men is a 'dirty secret', which goes unmentioned, unacknowledged or even denied.

The principal precipitant of binge eating and bulimia nervosa is simply extreme weight loss. Most men I have treated with bulimia nervosa have described a history of dieting. This works on both a physical and mental level. In physical terms, extreme dieting removes one's true awareness of hunger and satiety. Eventually you cannot trust your body to govern your behaviour. The eating behaviour then becomes governed by an external set of rules, often preposterous and unsustainable in nature, rather than by listening to what your body is telling you. However, most people who diet do not develop bulimia, whereas most people who develop bulimia will have dieted. In addition to this physical effect, the psychological impact of dieting becomes relevant. Men who develop bulimia nervosa are more likely to experience what have been termed 'cognitive distortions', in the way they think about themselves and the world around them. These are discussed in greater detail in Chapter 16 on cognitive therapy. They may think in very black-and-white terms, drawing arbitrary conclusions from quite minor events: 'She didn't talk to me today because she thinks I'm fat.' Negative events are seen as bigger than they really are (*magnification*): 'I'm earning less than my brother, and that means I'm a complete failure.' Or else positive events are neglected or underplayed: 'I may have just been awarded a 2:1 at university, but it doesn't alter the fact that people think I'm ugly and boring.'

When applied to dieting, the physiological impact of starvation is compounded by the psychological impact of this self-perception, almost hard-wired into the brain. Typically, rigid dietary rules are ever so slightly broken, to which the man with bulimia responds catastrophically. The good news is that we can influence these factors by the therapy known as 'cognitive therapy'. Later in the book, I will introduce you to the idea of 'learning to think straight' (Chapter 16).

Once the cycle of bingeing and vomiting has been established, it is then perpetuated by deep-rooted thoughts. These thoughts have been called 'schemata'. Schemata define how you think about yourself and judge yourself. Ultimately, an already fragile self-esteem is lowered by the cycle of bingeing and vomiting, and becomes a self-fulfilling prophecy. Feelings of powerlessness are compounded by the true loss of control that is bulimia nervosa. A fear of gaining weight prevents the sufferer from giving up the one aspect of their disorder that would most rapidly promote recovery, namely the compensatory behaviours. Finally, at a physical level, parts of the brain that control hunger and appetite, such as the hypothalamus, adapt to this odd pattern of extreme hunger and extreme satiation, such that terms like hunger no longer have any real meaning.

Chapter 5

Muscle dysmorphia (bigorexia)

A few years ago I wrote an article for the medical journal the *Lancet* that I entitled 'From Charles Atlas to the Adonis Complex – Fat Is More Than A Feminist Issue'. This was an attempt to make sense of the growing literature concerning a condition that had been named muscle dysmorphia. I strongly argued that the condition had many similarities to anorexia nervosa 'in reverse', and that treatments were needed which resembled those of eating disorders.

As with anorexia nervosa, muscle dysmorphia exists at the end of a spectrum of behaviours designed to reshape the body. While I have treated several men with muscle dysmorphia, I have seen several hundred young men who are dreadfully unhappy in their bodies and who are disabled by their compulsive exercise routines, yet don't quite fulfil the diagnostic criteria for the full condition.

Men have become trapped between the male 'body image industries' and their own inability to articulate their feelings. The media are not to blame: advertising is designed to sell, and sales are based on engendering dissatisfaction, ultimately equating happiness with shopping. That is what advertising is all about, and we can no more blame advertising or its medium, men's magazines, than to blame a frog for croaking. That is its purpose. However, we now live in a society in which the average male college student aspires to a body shape 14 kg more muscular than their actual, mimicking the common belief in women that they will be more attractive at a lower weight than their own. Just as most men still prefer Marilyn Monroe's size 16 figure, so most women reject the brawny monstrosities evident on the pages of so many men's magazines. Men and women are attracted by images of sustainable health. But the power of the body image industries to make us feel unhappy about ourselves continues unabated. In the USA, one in 15 male college students are abusing steroids. Steroid abuse comes at a high price. Over one in 20 men regularly taking steroids attempt suicide during steroid withdrawal.

Jack's story

Jack first consulted a psychiatrist reluctantly and only after his girlfriend presented him with an ultimatum. In technical terms, he was at a 'pre-contemplative stage' of motivation to change. He simply did not think he had a problem, and thought the problem was in others' attitudes to him. He told the following story:

I was a skinny kid, and very self-conscious about the way I looked. I particularly hated my knobbly knees and used to get teased at school about them. Things were fairly miserable at home in any case, so that was just one piece of the jigsaw.

I was really excited when I got a place at a good university, and I kind of tried to make myself into a different person. I didn't want to be seen as nerdy anymore, and started to think more about the way I dressed and my haircut. I even got my ear pierced. I would have been teased about things like that at school, but it was a lot easier where people didn't really know me.

I started working out in the university gym – after all, it was free and I didn't have much money. I found I was really good at lifting weights, and I surprised myself that I could shift heavier weights than guys who looked bigger than me. Three evenings a week I would hang out with them, and it felt good to be part of the crowd, though no one said much and there was always a sense of competition about who was biggest and strongest.

I really began to bulk out, particularly my biceps and pecs, though nothing I did seemed to make my spindly legs any bigger. Oddly the bigger I got, the more I wanted to grow. I became a lot more self-conscious about myself in the changing rooms, comparing myself with the other guys, thinking that their glutes and pecs seemed bigger than mine, even though I was lifting heavier weights.

I wasn't doing as well as I had hoped at uni, and almost flunked my first year. I managed to scrape a 2.2, but instead of being top of the class as I used to be, I was pretty mediocre academically. Going to the gym was my way of 'succeeding'. . . . I've always needed to feel 'simply the best' at something.

This will sound silly, but I started to work out at the same time as I was revising. I mean, I would have dumbbells next to the desk, and even a mirror, and I would do 30 minutes of revision followed by some biceps curls or squats. It felt good. Sometimes I would do this till 3 am, but feel tired the next day.

I began to be obsessed with my diet. I know it must seem strange to someone who doesn't understand these things. I used to try to eat lots of raw eggs, partly because they were really cheap and partly because I read about how useful they were in body building, though at that stage I didn't really know what I was doing. I would make this sort of mixture of raw eggs and milk and orange juice, and have it for breakfast, but then I would feel sick if I immediately did a work-out, so I started getting up earlier and earlier in the morning.

Some days I would skip lectures to fit the whole routine in, and some days I would get up dead early, like at four in the morning, just so I could manage the diet and exercise at the same time. Frankly it didn't actually make much difference, but it made me feel in control, as if my body was a machine. Then I began to read bodybuilding magazines and sent away for some [commercially available protein supplements].

It got to the point where I wanted to use free weights much more than the fixed weights, but there weren't really very many of them at the university gym, so I joined a gym in town that was full of really hard-core types. I felt very self-conscious going there the first time. I wore a long-sleeved sweat shirt and tracksuit bottoms, because I just felt like I was this skinny kid and they would all wonder what the hell I was doing there. That feeling didn't go away, but I began to feel like I had a right to be there. It was as if I was joining this elite. By now I just couldn't care less about my studies and only just started to keep my head above water. I used to avoid going home to see my mum and dad, partly because things were difficult there, but also because there wasn't a gym in this little village. I still had my old girlfriend from sixth form college, but I hardly saw her at all. I didn't go out with anyone at uni either. I said to myself that it was because I was being faithful, but I think it was really because I felt very self-conscious about the way I looked. I used to hate it when my girlfriend made comments about my appearance, even when she said nice things, and I don't know how she stuck by me.

I soon realised that everyone at the new gym was taking steroids. I was really terrified of that. I'm not stupid and I read all the stuff saying that they made your balls shrink and gave you cancer blah blah blah.

But the guys who were taking them didn't seem to have problems and I gave it a go. It was amazing. I started taking a pill . . ., and it just built me up to solid muscle. I could pump far more than I could ever pump before, and the effect was really rapid. But then I got hold of something . . ., which is actually a drug they give to horses! But you can get it just about anywhere. I started a cycle of injecting it, and it was incredible how much muscle weight I gained on just 2 cc twice a week, which was far less than the others were using. Not only did it pump up my chest and biceps, but I also found my legs were looking bulkier. It didn't have any bad effects at all. Some folks said they got spots, but I didn't have problems. Yes, my balls were a bit smaller, but as soon as I stopped a cycle they would grow back again, and so I just didn't believe anything I'd read before about steroids, it didn't make sense, and I thought it was all really about stopping guys cheating at the Olympics. What I really didn't like was the effect it had on my mind. It really began to mess with my mood, or at least that was what people told me, though I didn't believe it. I felt so angry. I used to cycle everywhere, and I remember one day the typical 'white van man' cut me up, but instead of just giving the V-signs I lost it, and punched the back of the van again and again. He got out for a fight, but I'd so obviously 'lost it' that he took one look at me and drove off as fast as he could.

I'd never had many friends in the house where I was living, but I became so peed off with everything that they couldn't stand me. I thought people were stealing my milk and bread and things like that. Well, they probably were, but I became really angry in a big way. I can just remember the look on the face of this one nerdy guy when I threatened him. He looked absolutely terrified, and the worst thing was that it made me feel *so* good, as if I was Rambo. At the time, I didn't really mind the *roid rage* as the way I felt after a cycle. I just felt so let down and depressed. I felt tired, tired, tired, and just couldn't get out of bed in the morning sometimes. I stopped getting essays in on time.

Eventually the university had had enough, and after several warnings they chucked me out. Can you believe it, I wasn't really bothered by being chucked out of university, but I was *really* concerned that I didn't know where to workout! That was the only thing that bothered me when I had to go back home to live with my parents. By then they had got their act together, and for the first time ever they managed to agree on something, with a little help from my girl.

I remember going home one day after swimming. I hated swimming. . . . It was so ineffective, but it was the only thing I could do to maintain my size and shape a little. Mum and Dad and Emma were sitting there, and they really gave me a talking to. I hadn't realised I was totally unbearable, and I blame the steroids for that. I wish someone had told me they messed more with your mind than your body. I still don't think pumping iron is a particular problem, but I could just about see their point of view about the steroids and my roid rage. That's why I agreed to see someone like you, and here I am.

It is important to distinguish muscle dysmorphia from working out or body building. Most men who go to gyms and pump iron do not have muscle dysmorphia. Muscle dysmorphia is diagnosed across three levels: the way people think (cognitions); the way this makes them behave; and the impact of this on their lives:

1   Cognition
   • the perception that your body is not sufficiently muscular
   • the drive to gain weight without gaining fat.
2   Behaviour
   • excessive exercise
   • dietary compulsions
   • use of performance-enhancing drugs
   • continuation of behaviour despite adverse outcome such as muscle injury.
3   Impact
   • A restricted repertoire of social/occupational activities.

But is muscle dysmorphia old wine in a new bottle? In 1969 an eminent psychiatrist, Sir Martin Roth, remarked on male body image disorders in men with a 'history of marked health consciousness and athleticism in which ardent devotion to athletic pursuits continued well beyond youth, as an over-compensation for real or imagined physical inferiorities'. Just as with anorexia and bulimia, muscle dysmorphia is probably not 'new' at all, but is certainly more common in our visual age.

Do you have muscle dysmorphia?

How do you know if you have muscle dysmorphia? Most folk who go to the gym and work out are perfectly healthy. As with anorexia and bulimia nervosa, this becomes an illness when it starts to cause harm. At the root of muscle dysmorphia is a distortion of body image. But, just as with anorexia and bulimia nervosa, many normal people have distortions to their self-perception without actually having an illness. The illness is defined not just by what you are thinking (Cognitions), but also what you are feeling (Affect) and doing (Behaviours). We have created a simple questionnaire, the MuD-Q, to address these three aspects of the illness (Box 5.1).

Take a few minutes out, and sit in a quiet room with a blank piece of paper. Remember that only you will read the answers. You should answer the questions spontaneously and intuitively, rather than thinking things through in too much detail. People who are suffering from muscle dysmorphia are good at deceiving themselves, and the more you think, the more you will try to whitewash over your authentic answers. Answer 'yes' or 'no'. Don't allow yourself to leave any blanks. Remember, no one else will read your answers when you've finished.

Box 5.1 MuD-Q: The Muscle Dysmorphia Questionnaire

1 Do you feel yourself to be scrawny when others tell you that you're too muscular?
Yes/No

2 Do you feel that you have lost control over your exercise regime?
Yes/No

3 Do physical activities to enhance your appearance dominate your life?
Yes/No

4 Do you spend more than an hour a day in training to improve your body shape?
Yes/No

5 Do you spend more than 30 minutes a day in checking your physical appearance?
Yes/No

6 Do you currently take drugs (steroids, diet pills, muscle-building agents) to enhance your physical appearance?
Yes/No

7 Do you regularly prioritise your physical regime over your career or studies?
Yes/No

8 Do you regularly prioritise your physical regime over your friends, family or relationships?
Yes/No

9 Have you continued in your physical regime despite being injured or ill?
Yes/No

10 Do you avoid situations in which your body will be seen by others?
Yes/No

Now, add up your score, giving yourself a 1 for every 'yes' and '0' for every 'no'. If you scored 5 or more (answered 'yes' to five or more of these questions) then it is highly probable you are suffering from muscle dysmorphia. If you answered 'yes' to three or more of these questions, then it is possible you are suffering from muscle dysmorphia.

An itch that can never be scratched

Academics, including myself, have debated the precise characteristics of muscle dysmorphia. Is it akin to anorexia nervosa? In a sense it is anorexia's flip-side – even with good muscle mass, sufferers believe their muscles are inadequate. Indeed newspapers and magazines have nicknamed it 'bigorexia' or 'reverse anorexia', and it certainly shares many behavioural and cognitive features of anorexia nervosa. Is it a form of obsessive-compulsive disorder (OCD)? People with muscle dysmorphia endlessly ruminate on thoughts of their body being too small and frail and undeveloped, and develop exercise rituals to placate those feelings.

Too often the condition is dismissed as vanity and narcissism, in flippant articles that ignore the genuine distress of the condition. People with muscle dysmorphia ask how they look not because they expect praise, but because they genuinely see themselves as scrawny. The body image distortion of anorexia nervosa, described in previous chapters, is just as powerful in muscle dysmorphia. The brain sees a perfectly normal body shape, but the mind perceives a skinny nobody, until personal identity is entirely wrapped up in the ability to gain weight, add muscle bulk and put flesh on the bones. But this is an itch that can never properly be scratched.

Thus the sufferer will endlessly work out, pumping iron to remedy the perceived smallness, performing resistance training, and exercising to excess. Exercise goes beyond the bounds of health. Sufferers will continue to train despite physical injury. They may take steroids or other muscle-building drugs to get bigger, sometimes with lethal consequences.

Just as we saw with anorexia nervosa, muscle dysmorphia is a full-time occupation. The body image distortion is always on your mind. The drive to gain weight is always the priority. Everything else must play second fiddle. Thus schooling, relationships and career will suffer. Self-loathing makes sexual relationships fraught, and it becomes much easier to avoid the messy arena of love altogether. Life in the gym is simple and straightforward. The aims and goals are clear-cut. It feels safer. But that safety is a fool's paradise.

What causes muscle dysmorphia?

We know less about muscle dysmorphia than anorexia nervosa or bulimia. We strongly suspect a genetic, biological element. In the same way that some people with anorexia are triggered into extreme weight loss by dieting, it appears that certain physiologies are at risk of muscle dysmorphia in response to over-exercise. Again comparable to anorexia nervosa and bulimia, psychological factors such as childhood teasing and past traumas seem to render people at risk. There seems to be a particular link to having witnessed your mother as a victim of domestic violence – the powerlessness of childhood being compensated by the exaggerated muscularity of adulthood.

There is a big overlap with depression – over half of all people with muscle dysmorphia have suffered from major depression. There is also an overlap with anorexia nervosa and bulimia. There is some overlap with anxiety. Almost a third have suffered from an anxiety disorder, such as social phobia (very extreme shyness). There is also an overlap with steroid abuse, but in most cases the use of steroids seems to stem from the muscle dysmorphia rather than vice versa. Finally, cultural factors create a climate in which 'heroic men' are portrayed as having excessively defined musculature. For a full description of muscle dysmorphia you can do no better than to read *The Adonis Complex* (see Appendix at the end of this book).

Treatment of muscle dysmorphia

Just like anorexia nervosa, muscle dysmorphia is an 'ego-syntonic' disorder. It isn't experienced as a problem, but as a solution to a problem. It is psychologically adaptive, though ultimately maladaptive. The sufferer will be reluctant to seek help, and often it is family or friends who will express concern.

Just as the person with anorexia nervosa is terrified of weight gain, so muscle dysmorphia sufferers are terrified of losing muscle bulk and withering away.

The acceptance of need for treatment comes gradually. Maybe family will persuade you to see a doctor or therapist. Maybe a major life event will bring the situation to a head. For many people with muscle dysmorphia, the disorder causes them to lose a friend or loved one, to lose their job or to suffer physical damage. There have been very few studies of treatments for muscle dysmorphia. Those that exist point towards the same treatments as anorexia nervosa and bulimia. The body image distortion and pattern of behaviours of men with muscle dysmorphia are strikingly analogous to those of men with anorexia nervosa. For that reason, I advocate the same seven-stage approach described in Part IV of this book.

What is the relationship between muscle dysmorphia and eating disorders?

Muscle dysmorphia is distinct from eating disorders, but the overlap is considerable. Some men with muscle dysmorphia will suffer from eating disorders, and more will have suffered from an eating disorder in the past. The characteristics of muscle dysmorphia are so close to those of eating disorders such as anorexia nervosa and bulimia as to almost represent a subclass. However, there is also considerable overlap between muscle dysmorphia and the conditions known as body dysmorphic disorder. Body dysmorphic disorder (BDD) is diagnosed in people who feel they have a disfigurement or defect in parts of their body despite evidence to the contrary.

There are significant elements of obsessive-compulsive behaviours in body dysmorphic disorder, and treatments usually combine the use of

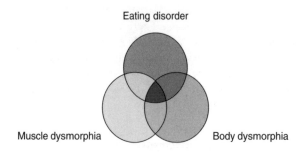

Figure 5.1 Relationship between eating disorders, muscle dysmorphia and body dysmorphia

medication with the use of psychotherapies specific to OCD. Why does it matter if muscle dysmorphia is closer to OCD or to eating disorders? What is the value of a diagnosis to a sufferer? Sometimes these arguments can seem hugely academic when you are suffering from distressing symptoms and want someone to make you feel better. But one purpose of a diagnosis is to suggest a course of action or treatment. The treatment of muscle dysmorphia and the treatment of eating disorders are similar, but different. Throughout this book, I have referred to both conditions separately, so as to highlight those differences. But the reality of the overlap between muscle dysmorphia and eating disorders is such that very often you will benefit from using all the strategies described in the book. The best way to convey this rather complex message is by a diagram. Figure 5.1 illustrates the potential for overlap between eating disorders, muscle dysmorphia and body dysmorphic disorder. Many men with muscle dysmorphia will have previously experienced bulimia, binge eating or anorexia nervosa, and in some instances the conditions coexist at the point of treatment.

Conclusion

Men are becoming increasingly concerned about body shape in this visual age. Women have suffered a disparity between the 'thin female beauty ideal' and biological reality for decades. Now men's body ideal is also drifting further away from biological health. The pursuit of excessive muscularity shares the same features as anorexia nervosa in terms of behaviours, thoughts and feelings. Effective treatments for muscle dysmorphia use the same approaches as eating disorder treatments.

Chapter 6

Obesity

Obesity places a heavy social, health and financial burden on our society. It has been estimated that obesity will bankrupt the UK's health service within the next ten years. Only recently have eating disorder specialists become interested in the management of obesity. It is beyond the remit of *The Invisible Man* to explore obesity in great depth, and this will be the subject of subsequent books. However, the overlap between anorexia nervosa, bulimia, binge eating and obesity can be considerable.

Obesity is not technically classified as a form of eating disorder, but undoubtedly it shares many features in common. For several years I provided psychological treatment for severely obese patients. In some instances obesity and anorexia nervosa appeared to be two sides of the same coin. Furthermore, men with eating disorders are much more likely to have been obese in the past than women. Fighting fat is therefore particularly pertinent to men with eating disorders.

Defining the problem

The body mass index (BMI) represents the normal standard for assessing weight. BMI represents weight (in kilograms) divided by height squared (in metres). Someone is considered overweight if their body mass index lies in the range of 25 to 30, and men are classed as obese if their body mass index is over 30. Cases of obesity have quadrupled in the last two decades, and almost one in five men is considered obese.

Obesity is linked to a wide range of health difficulties including cardiac disease, diabetes, strokes and arthritis. Our brains are hardwired to be more sensitive to hunger than satiety, and in a culture that exposes us to unlimited food resources it is unsurprising that so many achieve a state of obesity. Furthermore, the battle against obesity lends itself to development of eating disorders. In clinical practice I have treated patients who have moved from obesity to bulimia to anorexia, and back again.

In men, fat tends to congregate in certain specific parts of the body and particularly waist, chest and buttocks. Too much fat around the abdomen (a typical 'beer belly') represents a specific risk to health. Recently doctors have been exploring a 'new' condition known as the 'metabolic syndrome', in which the combination of overweight, poor glucose control akin to diabetes, high blood pressure and cardiovascular disease conspires to create a high risk of sudden death. Thus a high BMI is not the only criteria for concern. It is an amalgam of health difficulties that are relevant, and the 'beer gut' predicts these.

It can therefore be more helpful to use someone's waist measurement rather than their absolute BMI. A 37-inch waist (94 cm) would represent overweight, with a 40-inch waist (102 cm) representing obesity. On the whole, being overweight does not matter so much if you are otherwise healthy and fit, and most of *The Invisible Man* is focused on men who believe they are overweight when they are actually perfectly normal.

What is the cause of obesity?

This is a difficult question to answer simply. At one extreme, some obese men are simply genetically predetermined. This probably accounts for at least a quarter of all obese men. Specific genes have been identified which control eating behaviour. One set of genes is linked to a hormone known as leptin, abnormalities in which will inevitably lead to obesity. The Pima Indians are a group whose genes will almost certainly cause them to develop obesity. Comparably, obesity can run in families.

At the other extreme, obesity can arise solely from the same psychological conflicts found in anorexia nervosa and bulimia nervosa. For these people, obesity indeed appears to be a form of eating disorder. More typically, it is multifactorial. Men move into obesity through a combination of their genes, mental state, physical disease or lifestyle changes. For example, someone genetically vulnerable to obesity may take a sedentary and stressful job, and begin to comfort eat or binge on alcohol to cope with stress. To blame the obesity on any one of these factors would be inaccurate. To address the obesity by purely one intervention, such as psychotherapy, would be insufficient. What is generally needed is an integrated approach combining changes in lifestyle, exercise and stress management.

A brief history of obesity

Many years ago we associated obesity with health. This sprang from an era when food was a scarce resource, such that signs of overweight were signs of affluence, power and success. The Venus of Willendorf, a fertility symbol from *c.* 24,000–22,000 BC, was an early icon of this (Figure 6.1).

In medieval times the 'plump' man was seen as jovial, friendly and respectable. For men in particular, overweight was a display of social solidity. By the twentieth century, research on obesity was more interested

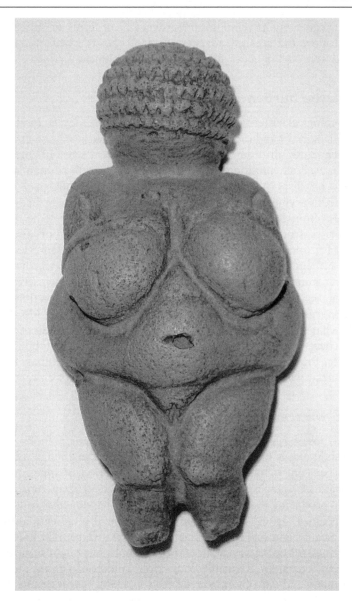

Figure 6.1 The Venus of Willendorf

in medical than psychological connotations. There was an explosion of 'basic science' research addressing genes and hormones, but psychological aspects were entirely neglected, to the point that obesity seemed to become a 'forgotten' eating disorder. More recently this has been rectified, including a consensus statement from the National Institute for Health that 'obesity creates an enormous psychological burden . . . in terms of suffering, this burden may be the greatest adverse effect of obesity'. Unfortunately this integrated approach has not filtered down into clinical services.

What is the burden of obesity?

The psychological suffering of the obese occurs at three levels. First, there is an intrinsic social handicap. Second, there is the burden of shame. Third, there is the eating disorder burden, exemplified by a sense of total loss of control, as well as emotional triggers to eating. The obese man wears his pathology on display to the outside world. An alcoholic may hide the problem from prying eyes, but the obese have no such hiding place. Already low self-esteem is further eroded by societal attitudes. For some men their obesity arises from a background of childhood trauma or abuse. The threshold for tolerating such abuse is lowered by this low self-esteem, such that the sufferer becomes trapped in a cycle of abuse in which they are forced to tolerate psychological or physical attacks upon themselves out of a sense of their own 'worthlessness', and that sense of worthlessness is simply confirmed by those attacks. In simpler terms, there is a loss of pride.

Studies have suggested that obesity is perceived as more disabling than deafness, heart disease, dyslexia, diabetes or even leg amputation. Society stigmatises the overweight, and there is clear evidence that they are disadvantaged when it comes to employment or university entrance.

How do we treat obesity?

Aiming to lose large amounts of weight very rapidly is a fool's strategy. Rapid weight loss is rarely sustained, and it is far better to aim at a limited loss of 5 per cent of body weight over a long period of time, through a combination of changes in lifestyle and diet, rather than extreme calorific restriction producing more intense weight loss, which nonetheless will either not be sustained, or will itself lead into development of an eating disorder.

In a typical weight loss regime, one may aim at a target of 1 lb (0.5 kg) a week, through subtle dietary changes. For example, one might substitute fats with fruit or vegetables. Reducing your alcohol intake can do far more good than the many and varied commercial diets available. Most people who are obese will consume far larger portion sizes than is normal, yet may be quite unaware of this. Changing the size of your plate in order to delineate the portion size of your dietary intake can sometimes be a helpful strategy.

Exercise does not appear terribly effective for weight loss, if you judge progress purely in terms of the weight. However, exercise is extremely effective in other ways. First, regular physical activity redistributes weight quite quickly, giving a better sense of rapid progress than is achieved through diet alone. Second, the physical benefits are considerable: a fit but fat person has lower morbidity and mortality than an unfit but less fat person. Third, many people who have achieved a state of obesity have quite lost touch with their true sense of hunger and satiety. Exercise can help reconnect with this sense. Fourth, a modest amount of regular exercise can operate as an antidepressant, giving you the motivation and drive to pursue the other steps necessary for weight loss.

The combination of modest physical activity and diet is probably the best approach to obesity in the initial stages, particularly where the exercise follows a period of several weeks of dietary restriction. Often it is better to aim at sustainable physical activity than pursue a fitness programme that is simply impractical. Walking to the bus stop, avoiding the lift, or taking the dog for a walk can all be more effective than joining a gym. A good gym can motivate, but all too often people become disillusioned and demoralised in their fitness regimes. For men who are overweight to the point of struggling with weight-bearing activities, swimming can be particularly beneficial. Many patients I have treated for obesity have seemed to benefit physically and also psychologically from swimming, reconnecting with and remembering their slimmer body.

Formal treatments of obesity

There are three formal treatment approaches used by doctors in the management of obesity. They are not mutually exclusive, and indeed are often best employed together.

Psychological treatments

For some people who are obese, specific psychotherapies can be effective in the treatment of their overweight. Cognitive behavioural therapy and interpersonal therapy are employed in much the same way as described elsewhere for bulimia. An important subgroup of people who are obese will have achieved that state through the regular pattern of binge eating described elsewhere in the book. Addressing binge eating through psychotherapy can be effective in weight loss. Restoring a sense of autonomy and self-esteem is also critical. Psychodynamic psychotherapies may be helpful here. Psychological approaches to the treatment of obesity may not result in miraculous quantified weight loss. However, for those people who are obese for psychological reasons, it is often a necessary, though not always sufficient, step before considering other treatments.

We addressed these factors in a range of published research in which we examined psychological variables as predictors of outcome in other forms of treatment. For those people with untreated binge eating or depression, non-psychological treatments were simply ineffective. It would be unwise for me to suggest that psychological therapies are the key to weight loss.

Weight loss is simply achieved through either decreased energy intake or increased energy expenditure. However, if you have developed a pattern of binge eating in response to stressful circumstances, reinforced by the hard-wiring of your brain that thinks in 'black and white', then until you have addressed those behaviours and cognitions, there is little point in dieting. Indeed, there is evidence that dieting may worsen binge eating.

Finally, a specific form of psychotherapy known as motivational enhancement therapy is helpful in making other treatment approaches succeed. We are currently studying a combination of interpersonal psychotherapy and motivational enhancement therapy as one integrated approach.

Medical treatments

In the past, a huge array of drugs was prescribed to people who were overweight as a means of weight manipulation. A 'cottage industry' sprang up of private slimming clinics prescribing these drugs. Most of them were based around the drug amphetamine, and it became apparent that the risks far outweighed the benefits. Amphetamine-based slimming pills can damage the heart and circulation, particularly causing raised blood pressure in the system of circulation between the heart and lungs. The prescription of such substances is now not permitted in the UK, but still goes on.

It is still relevant to prescribe some 'weight control' drugs, and these remain available for some people who are obese, particularly where other dietetic approaches have not succeeded. They do not work on their own, but only in combination with diet and exercise. One such drug is orlistat, which operates in the gut by stopping absorption of fat. High fat content foods will result in unpleasant side effects and so people taking orlistat are required to maintain a diet which is low in fat. For many people with obesity this can be quite difficult, but where there is motivation, then it can help in a broader strategy of weight loss.

Sibutramine is a drug that acts on the brain to suppress appetite, by changing the brain's levels of the chemicals noradrenalin and serotonin. Like orlistat, sibutramine is only useful in combination with behavioural, dietetic and exercise regimes. Because of its side effects, it is necessary to monitor the impact on the heart and blood pressure in the early stages, and it is avoided in obese men who have previous histories of eating disorders or major depression.

Surgery

Surgery is becoming an increasingly popular choice for people with severe morbid obesity, and indeed has been recommended in new guidelines from the National Institute for Health and Clinical Excellence (NICE), where 'there are no psychosocial contraindications'. Two basic approaches are taken. In the first, a gastric band is placed around the stomach and linked to a small bulb implanted just beneath the skin. By means of injecting fluid in or out of that bulb, the band can be tightened or loosened. Adjustable gastric banding can be highly successful, and is usually implemented by the most modern laparoscopic surgical techniques. This means that complications of anaesthesia are minimised, and often people are discharged from hospital after such an operation following one night only. The technique requires a high degree of skill on the part of the surgeon, and one would seek such surgery only from an accomplished and experienced clinician. The gastric band causes people to reduce the portion size of their food intake, and thereby adapt to the band. In a sense this therefore is working as a form of enforced 'behaviour therapy', assisting in the relearning of a more normal eating pattern. For this to work, a patient must be motivated, insightful and capable of such change. This means that gastric banding surgery is not a simple one-off procedure, but requires quite intensive surgical, and often psychological, follow-up.

Our research suggests that roughly a quarter of patients seeking this form of intervention are unsuitable without first addressing their psychological morbidity. For example, this may involve cognitive behavioural therapy for binge eating disorder.

A second category of surgical approaches involves stomach bypass, whereby the gut is 'replumbed' to reduce absorption of calories. This represents more major surgery than a gastric band, but can be suitable in patients who are less able to modify their behaviour. The corollary I have used in the past is that gastric banding is like taking someone who has previously been able to ride a bicycle, but has forgotten how to balance. By using stabilisers, lowered or raised, you gradually relearn your sense of balance until you no longer need the stabilisers at all. This is akin to gastric banding surgery in which the band can be tightened or loosened according to the patient's progress, until they relearn a normal pattern of eating.

However, some people are simply unable to ride a bike, and in that instance a tricycle is an alternative. This gives a more guaranteed outcome, but is possibly more intrusive and less flexible than the alternative. Similarly gastric bypass is suitable for people who are less able to relearn a normal eating pattern. With all forms of surgery, some degree of capacity to change eating behaviour is necessary, and there are some patients with morbid obesity whose psychological issues render them unsuitable for any surgery whatsoever, or who require psychological treatments before pursuing surgery.

The story of Sam

Sam was a 45-year-old man who presented in a wheelchair. Twenty years of obesity had caused his knees to be damaged with arthritis. As his mobility decreased, so did he become more sedentary and his weight gain escalated.

He was unable to continue in his job, becoming miserable and later suffering from major depression. In his misery he would binge on large amounts of junk food, particularly in the evenings when he felt most lonely and vulnerable. He supplemented his binge eating with a regular consumption of at least two bottles of wine a day. When he first presented for treatment, he was frankly a mess; dependent on alcohol, suffering from a depressive illness and requiring surgery for his knees, yet unsuitable for such surgery because of the anaesthetic risk he posed.

Yet his friends believed him to be the 'life and soul' of the party. He maintained a superficial veneer of 'the jovial fat man', and his friends teased him mercilessly about his body shape, without meaning to be cruel, and without realising the extent to which this damaged his already fragile self-esteem.

In the past he had attempted to lose weight by extreme measures, which reflected his tendency to think dichotomously: 'If I am not having a "thin day", then I must be having a "fat day".' He would try to eat absolutely nothing all day long, and then succumb to absolute starvation in the early evening. He sought a simple 'quick fix' to his problems by requesting surgery. However, the surgeon was a brilliant clinician, as adept in considering psychological and medical as surgical issues. Before agreeing to operate, Sam required a series of preparatory steps. First, his dependence on alcohol trumped all his other problems. As long as Sam was perpetually drunk, he was unlikely to be able to change anything else in his life. His physical as well as psychological dependence on alcohol required medical treatment with particular prescribed drugs, and subsequent psychological treatment.

Of course, he was drinking because of his depression, and that too required formal treatment over a 12-month period. After a significant improvement in his mood, he was now able to consider the psychological issues that had perpetuated his disordered eating. By now this eloquent, intelligent man had gleaned tremendous insight into his own inner world. He eagerly engaged in cognitive behavioural therapy for his eating disorder, and thereby managed to stabilise his eating pattern and desist from binge eating altogether.

In itself, the combination of a reduction in alcohol and the cessation of binge eating resulted in a modest but significant weight loss. This was not the aim of the treatment, but the stabilisation of his mood and eating was a necessary prerequisite for other treatments. Even this modest weight loss produced a dramatic improvement in his quality of life. His mobility improved slightly, so he was able to take up swimming, and was occasionally mobile without his wheelchair. Medical complications of his obesity, including high blood pressure, also improved quite dramatically after relatively modest weight loss, and he no longer had to take a cocktail of prescribed drugs, which had caused him some unpleasant side effects.

After 18 months of preparatory treatment, Sam received surgery, which was successful and uncomplicated. He received regular follow-up from the surgical team, which not only addressed physical maters but also considered his eating behaviours and emotional consequences. Eventually his weight loss permitted him knee surgery. His mobility improved dramatically. As the final stage in his rehabilitation, he was able to return to work.

You can see from the story of Sam that a single approach to his overweight would have been fruitless. Eating disorder specialists, dieticians, physicians or surgeons alone would have made very little difference. What was required was an integrated approach combining all aspects of treatment in a seamless package of care.

More men than women with eating disorders have a past history of obesity. Often obesity and eating disorders represent two sides of the same coin. Psychological treatments of obesity can produce modest but real benefits, and are often a prerequisite of lifestyle approaches, as well as the medical and surgical treatments described above. A holistic biopsychosocial approach is best, and quick fixes are nothing but attractive illusions.

Part III

Science fiction and science fact

Chapter 7

What causes body image disorders in men?

Beware unifactorial dogma

There may be as many causes of body image disorders as there are men who have those disorders, but we do know something of the general causes. Forming any understanding of the origin of your own problem can be critical in combating it. However, answering the question of what causes body image disorders is quite tricky. The causes of eating disorders are multifactorial. There are factors that may render you vulnerable to the risk of developing a disorder (predisposing factors). There are factors which commonly precipitate you into a pattern of disordered eating or shape manipulation. Finally, there are those factors which perpetuate that problem. Rather than looking at a single factor, eating disorder specialists usually formulate an understanding of the condition by means of this model of predisposing, precipitating and perpetuating factors.

One must be very cautious in accepting unifactorial dogmatic theories. For example, it is perfectly plausible to imagine that changing images of men portrayed in the media might be at the root of the growing epidemic of male eating problems. However, it may be simplistic to blame those images for an individual's eating disorder. Simplicity is very attractive when you have an illness but, in my opinion, it is rarely helpful to the individual sufferer to suggest that their eating disorder is the result of genes, culture, traumatic events or dieting. All of the above may be relevant, but it is the subtle combination of predisposing, precipitating and perpetuating factors which is important. Beware the unifactorial dogma.

Predisposing factors

High achievers – simply the best

Our temperament or personality is with us from cradle to grave. Just like our physical bodies, our temperaments come in all shapes and sizes. We welcome the variety of personalities in society, and a healthy society has a place, or a role, for everyone. When we have studied the personalities of men vulnerable to developing body image and eating disorders, we find some consistent patterns. First, many of the men have suffered from chronically low self-esteem. This may have been apparent as far back as childhood, and may have been the result of events in childhood. It may simply be the genetic make-up of the individual, or more often it is a combination of the two.

The tendency to denigrate yourself, to view nothing as 'good enough', becomes hardwired into your brain, affecting the way you think and analyse the world. For example, a man with an eating disorder may have done far better than his friends at school and gone on to achieve professional success, but might instead focus on the fact that he is less successful than his brother or father. The 'cup half empty' phenomenon is one aspect of one of the most effective therapies in eating disorders, known as cognitive therapy.

Many men with eating disorders are perfectionists by nature, sometimes to the point of obsessionality. They strive for excellence and often achieve it. The best is not good enough, but instead they seek better than the best. Current fashions in the media tap into this perfectionism and insecurity. It is no longer sufficient to be simply successful in your job. You have to cook like a super chef, look like a super model, and spend like the super rich. The combination of a naturally perfectionist temperament and the exploitation of male insecurity in our contemporary culture creates a potent brew. Even more potent is the cocktail of low self-esteem and perfectionism. One without the other can be manageable, but when the two are combined it is a recipe for unhappiness. The transient and ineffective resolution of that unhappiness is achieved through the manipulation of weight or shape.

Of course, not every man with an eating disorder has low self-esteem or perfectionism. Likewise, not every person with low self-esteem and perfectionism goes on to develop an eating disorder. Scratch the surface of every successful individual, and you will find at least a trace of these elements. Striving for perfection and being dissatisfied with your immediate achievements is the very fuel of success in life. That is why so many men with body image problems are high achievers. Many of my patients come from successful walks of life. Lawyers, doctors, journalists, teachers, academics and athletes – all are notable for personalities combining this drive for perfection and dissatisfaction with what they have achieved so far. Perhaps it is unsurprising that eating disorders and body image problems are greatly over-represented in the most successful men in our society.

So what is to be done about it? You can no more change your personality than a leopard can change its spots. Indeed, it is probably very harmful to try to be something you are not. The secret is not to try to change but to channel, to recognise your personality and thereby channel it into a more fruitful outlet than eating disorder or body image problems. Instead of managing the dissatisfaction through conflict with food, weight and shape, successful therapy aims to help you channel your personality into a more creative and fruitful outlet. Instead of being the world's best anorectic, or having the biggest pecs in the gym, you strive to achieve personal and professional success. Of course it is far simpler to focus energies on calorie counting or working out in the gym than to battle it out in the professional world or deal with problems in a relationship, but the insight you glean from understanding your personality will motivate you to abandon the simplicity of the eating disorder in favour of the complexity of these superior challenges.

All in the genes?

Year on year, we form a deeper understanding of the genetic basis of eating disorders and body image problems. We can study the genetics of eating disorders in two ways: by looking at families and by looking at twins. The more we study, the more complicated it gets. However, the simple fact is that we do indeed know that genes play a significant part in your vulnerability to an eating problem. This does not necessarily mean there is a 'gene' for anorexia nervosa, bulimia or muscle dysmorphia. We know that if you have a close relative with an eating disorder you have at least three times the risk of developing an eating disorder yourself. It is also true that families vulnerable to depression and alcohol abuse will be more likely to generate men with eating disorders.

Thus we have a clear idea of the 'whats', but not yet of the 'whys' or 'wherefores'. For example, is it the fact that your genes determine your risk of an eating disorder in particular, or do your genes lay down the seeds from which that eating disorder grows? To give you an example, as I discussed above, temperament and personality are important factors in some people with eating disorders. We now know that personality traits are quite hereditary. Could it be the genetics of that vulnerable personality that are passed on from parent to boy? Comparably, we know that certain body shapes and sizes have a genetic basis. Could it be that these factors have a particular impact? Finally, we know that essential chemicals in the brain, and particularly the chemical known as serotonin, play an important part in the origins of eating disorders. There is some evidence that men with anorexia nervosa may have a genetic predisposition to abnormalities in this chemical system. The jury is out.

Of course you cannot change your genes. But what the understanding of genes permits is a process of self-evaluation. Just as some folk have a genetic propensity to develop diabetes, and thereby may need to make changes in their lifestyle accordingly, so some men may have a genetic propensity to develop eating disorders, and so may need to protect and inoculate themselves against other risk factors which are under their control.

Depression and anxiety

Depression is very common in people who suffer from eating disorders. For many the depression is simply secondary to the eating problem. It is unsurprising that the sorrow and suffering of anorexia nervosa or muscle dysmorphia may result in a deep and profound melancholia. Likewise, nutrition plays an important part in mood, and symptoms of depression are very common in all causes of starvation. However, it is also the case that an important minority of patients with eating disorders have developed depression prior to their eating disorders. In this instance, the pattern of disordered eating can be a response to the low mood. Just as some alcoholics will drink to deal with their depression, so some men with eating disorders will be trying to resolve a primary problem of melancholia.

Several years ago we tried to quantify all of this in a research study. We examined levels of depression in patients admitted for the treatment of anorexia nervosa. We found that weight gain was accompanied by a lowering of mood, such that most patients in early recovery from anorexia nervosa passed through a clinically significant episode of existential despair. This is of more than academic interest. If the eating disorder or muscle dysmorphia is being used to dampen down feelings of despair and depression, then treating that eating disorder seems to increase those negative feelings. In more basic terms, if you engage in treatment for your eating disorder you may well feel worse before you feel better. Knowing that these periods of depression are temporary is quite important if you are to tolerate them. Indeed, one of the features common to the many and varied psychotherapies used in the treatment of eating disorders is simply a process of becoming 'sadder and wiser'. Another is learning the ability to put your feelings into words rather than behaviours. It is therefore unsurprising that there is a strong link between depression and disordered eating.

Of course depression is not the only mood disorder that has been linked to eating disorders. A significant minority of patients with eating disorders suffer from a range of anxiety problems, including obsessional-compulsive symptoms as well as an array of phobias. The overlap between eating disorders and obsessive compulsive disorders is so great that some people have suggested that eating disorders are merely a manifestation of obsessional behaviour. This remains speculative, simplistic and most probably untrue. Nonetheless, very many men with eating disorders develop rituals and fears which need to be tackled in addition to the disordered eating.

Weight problems

More men than women with body image disorders will have grappled with overweight prior to the onset of their illness. It is quite common to see an eating disorder or muscle dysmorphia developing in a man who has been slightly overweight as a boy. Take the following example:

Martin came from a happy stable family. Martin's dad was a well-built muscular man who liked his food and his beer. The family enjoyed mealtimes and often over-indulged. Martin grew into a rather plump young boy. At primary school some of the other kids made comments about this, and for a couple of years his nickname was 'Fat Face'. However, he was not really distressed by this, and the comments were made amiably. He was a popular boy at primary school and, despite his shape and weight, was always very good at sport. That seemed to make a difference.

Things changed when he was sent to a big secondary school. He didn't really know the people there, and from the first day they began to tease him about his weight. They called him 'the fat shit' and even some of the teachers joined in the laughter. As his body began to develop and he grew interested in girls, he became acutely self-conscious about his shape and weight. In the bigger school, he was no longer regarded as much of an athlete, and was generally relegated to the third or fourth teams.

Because he was so upset, his mother took him to the GP about his weight. The GP told him he was fat and needed to lose weight, but didn't really tell him how he should do this. He was referred to a dietician but the waiting list was over one year long. Instead, Martin put himself on an odd diet whereby he ate only cereal for breakfast, lunch and dinner. He would avoid the family meals he had previously enjoyed so much, and his parents didn't know how to handle the situation. They watched helplessly as he wasted away.

The more weight he lost, the better he felt and, once he started to look skeletal, the boys at school simply left him alone. They almost seemed scared of him. He much preferred this to the negative attention he had been getting. By the age of 15 he was nothing but 'skin and bone'. One day he fainted at the bus stop and was taken to see the doctor, who immediately had him admitted to a medical ward with severe anorexia nervosa.

The above narrative exemplifies the complexity of looking at what causes an eating disorder. You could not pin Martin's anorexia nervosa on obesity alone. It was the subtle combination of his childhood overweight, extreme dieting, his isolation and bullying at school and possibly his parents' timidity in taking charge of his problem.

It has also been suggested that the link between overweight and eating disorders is biological. Recently we have come to understand a hormone known as leptin as being relevant in some people who are overweight. Leptin is a hormone that controls feeding behaviour via its action on the brain. Some very rare individuals have genetic abnormalities in their levels of leptin, which mean they will inevitably become overweight. (This is discussed in Chapter 6 when we look at obesity.) However, direct links between leptin abnormalities and eating disorders have proven elusive. In one of the first studies of leptin and anorexia nervosa, we examined levels of serum leptin during weight gain in anorexia nervosa, and found that they were really no different to the comparable changes in people who did not have anorexia nervosa. However, it is possible that some men with anorexia nervosa or bulimia may have abnormalities in the way that leptin, and related chemicals, acts on the brain in some individuals. This may be particularly true in men who go on extreme diets. It is possible that there might be a direct biological link between obesity and anorexia or bulimia. Research into the biology of eating disorders is at an exciting stage.

Trauma

A significant minority of men with eating disorders or muscle dysmorphia may have experienced severe traumas either in their childhood or early adulthood. Human nature can cope quite well with one-off traumatic events, but repeated trauma can have a profound impact. For example, if someone mugs you at the bus stop, you will probably feel very anxious for a few weeks, but then put it behind you and get on with your life. However, if you get mugged every month, or beaten up by your dad every Saturday night, it begins to get under your skin and change you as a person, altering the way you see yourself and the world around you. It even changes the wiring in your brain, as the brain adapts to constant fear.

Some men develop eating disorders as a response to traumatic events, particularly of a repetitive nature. To date, the main focus of research on trauma and eating disorders has been around the issue of sexual abuse. It is undoubtedly true that men with eating disorders are more likely to have suffered sexual abuse in childhood. But most men who have been abused as children do not develop eating disorders, and most men with eating disorders have not been abused. Nonetheless, there can be a significant overlap.

It is critical not to be oversimplistic with these matters. Some therapists wrongly seek hidden histories of sexual abuse in every man presenting with an eating disorder, and this is unhelpful and distorted. Similarly, uncovering a history of abuse is not the end of the matter. Having experienced a traumatic event is less important than the quality, context and chronicity of that event. A good therapist would see beyond the mere presence or absence of a traumatic event, and try to understand its meaning.

Male victims of sexual abuse are less common than women, but when it occurs it can be particularly complex. There is an underreporting of sexual abuse among men and boys, and this appears to arise from a heightened shame and stigmatisation in comparison with women. As most perpetrators of sexual abuse are men, abused boys may suffer issues of gender identity uncertainty. This adds to the complexity of recovery, and one simple 'solution' to disturbances of gender identity is to switch off your hormones altogether by developing an eating disorder. Thus, in a very few cases, an eating disorder may arise as a way of coping with the complex ramifications of trauma.

Of course sexual abuse is not the only trauma suffered by boys who later develop eating disorders. Severe physical and psychological bullying is common among boys, and they may react by trying to manipulate their body into a different shape. Many young lads go through a period of hero worshipping action heroes and bodybuilders, and in part this may be driven by society's expectations of boys. Real men don't cry. You either have sand kicked in your eyes or you do the kicking. Physical prowess becomes a means of protecting yourself from being a victim, instead identifying with the aggressor. Society itself grapples with concepts of masculinity. So it is entirely unsurprising that a bullied teenager may also be confused about what is expected of them, and resort to cartoon representations of what it means to be a man.

Families

Twenty years ago it was suggested that certain types of families were more likely to have children that would develop schizophrenia. Styles of parenting were blamed for a condition that is now largely regarded as being biological. In the meantime, these parents experienced shame and guilt at what was seen as being 'their problem'. We need to learn from these lessons when we approach families in eating disorders. Blaming families for an eating disorder is rarely true, and never helpful. There are suggestions that certain types of families are more likely to give rise to eating disorders than others. For example, families of men who develop anorexia nervosa have been described as 'consensus sensitive'. This means that the rules of the family are rigidly set, arguments are avoided and agreement is presented on the surface, even if there are many disagreements underneath the water. Of course it is extremely hard to know whether the family dynamics cause those eating disorders, or whether instead the family is reacting to a child with a serious illness.

Speaking from personal clinical experience, most of the men I have treated with eating disorders have had loving, nurturing, kind and considerate families. A significant minority have had problems beyond their control, including bereavements and impact of grief on the surviving parents. An even smaller minority have had more significant persistent abnormalities that might have actually helped to cause the problem in the first place.

However, far more common is the problem of how the family reacts. Having a son with anorexia, bulimia or muscle dysmorphia is a horrible predicament. There is no 'rule book' to tell you how you should or should not behave with your son. Sometimes families say or do the wrong things for the best of motives. They may collude with the illness, by adapting their lives around the idiosyncrasies of the sufferer. They may react in ways that are meant to be helpful, but are perceived as aggressive and threatening. They may simply not know what to do at all, and therefore appear to be uncaring or distant.

In conclusion, families are rarely the cause of the problem, though this may be true in some instances. However, universally, families can be the solution to the problem. We know for a fact that family interventions are a particularly effective remedy. It can be powerful for a therapist to recruit family members as co-therapists, and disastrous to work in opposition. A good therapist will help families understand how best to assist at critical stages in recovery. Sometimes all it takes is sitting in a room and talking. If you have an eating disorder, it may be helpful to tell your mum, dad or partner the things they do which you find helpful and the things they do which you find unhelpful. You are their best guide.

Culture

Culture provides an enormous influence over body image disorders. Over 20 years ago, Garner and Garfinkel studied images of beauty portrayed in women's magazines, and found a highly significant trend towards a thinner, tubular standard. This set the scene for understanding the origins of female eating disorders in cultural terms. Later, comparable trends were identified among gay men, and now we are beginning to see the same influences among all young men. Recently we carried out studies on young male university students, suggesting that body image disparagement is rife.

All about sex – sexual confusion, sexual identity?

Most men with body image disorders are straight, and most gay men do not have body image disorders. Let us get that fact out of the way. Nonetheless, roughly one in five men with eating disorders have a homosexual orientation. It is easy to attempt to explain this by speaking of the 'gay' culture, but there are as many gay cultures as there are straight cultures, and one becomes simplistic in such descriptions. It is certainly true that for some gay men a focus on body shape and weight can become quite pathological. To put it in perspective, more straight women than gay men suffer body image disparagement, but likewise gay men are more likely to experience this than straight men. It is therefore unsurprising that gay men are at heightened risk of eating disorders and muscle dysmorphia, but gender orientation is not a comprehensive explanation.

There is a huge difference between sexual confusion and sexual orientation. Most gay men have no confusions whatsoever, are confident and certain in their orientation. Some straight, gay and bisexual men pass through periods in their lives where they are confused over issues of sexuality. An otherwise straight man might be attracted to another man. Likewise, a gay man might fall in love with a woman. It is these issues of sexual confusion, rather than sexual orientation, which can be a complex feature of a minority of men with eating disorders.

Starving yourself becomes an apparent solution to the problem. Once you begin to lose weight your body changes physically, in ways which resemble a passage from puberty back into childhood. Hormones dwindle, testosterone levels fall, and the low weight adult male with anorexia nervosa will have the physiology of a prepubescent. For a small minority of men with anorexia nervosa in particular, the disorder helps them resolve sexual confusion by ridding them of sexuality. On the other hand, successful treatment reverses the situation. Some men with anorexia nervosa have described the process of recovery as re-experiencing puberty. Puberty is a messy business, and so it is unsurprising that recovery can be very difficult.

Having a forum to discuss issues of sexuality, where relevant, can be quite important in the treatment of eating disorders and muscle dysmorphia. This is not always easy on units with predominantly female staff. However, there is also a risk of taking these issues to an extreme. Some health-care professionals look for sexual issues in all men with eating disorders, where they are simply not relevant. So, in case any health care professionals are reading this book, I will end with a clear message:

- Most men with body image disorders are straight.
- A significant minority are gay.
- Most gay men are happy and confident in their sexuality.
- A significant minority of men, straight and gay, with body image disorders have issues of confusion in their sexuality, which need to be resolved.
- Most do not!

Precipitating factors

All the previous issues represent a background of vulnerability from which a body image disorder may emerge. However, what do we know of the factors which may plunge someone into a fully fledged illness?

Dieting

Dieting is the most frequently destabilising factor in men who develop eating disorders. This can work at several different levels. Diets can confuse our brains, which have developed a better sensitivity to hunger than satiety. The part of the brain known as the hypothalamus directs this. Some men who develop eating disorders will have a history of onset associated with dieting, though most men who do diet do not then develop eating disorders. Current research is examining whether certain men are biologically pre-destined to develop eating disorders in response to dieting. For some, it is like 'a switch being turned on', either through weight loss spiralling out of control, or the cycle of binging and purging digging its claws into you.

Dieting also provides a potent source of 'reward', which can be quite addictive. In the initial stages, you may experience positive comments. You may feel a profound sense of personal achievement. Emotions may be contained.

Life events

Other factors are equally relevant in the precipitation of eating disorders in men. The onset of puberty is a common precipitant. Its potential impact has already been characterised in the narrative above concerning Martin. Puberty is a complex amalgam of psychological and physiological changes, and the ability of an eating disorder to reverse puberty both psychologically and physiologically can seem quite attractive. Puberty is also a time of intense change. Relationships within families can change markedly. One's relationship with one's own body and identity also changes quite markedly. This flux is experienced as disturbing for some individuals, and an eating disorder or muscle dysmorphia can be a simplified means of resolving the situation. Puberty is also a time at which we move from the simpler rules of childhood into the more complex rules of adult relations, particularly thinking of sexual relationships. The whole messy business of dating can make the comfort of an eating disorder quite attractive. Finally, many men who develop eating disorders do so as a result of any major life event such as a significant trauma, the loss of someone you love or leaving home for the first time.

Perpetuating factors

Once you have developed an eating disorder, what keeps it going? We know there are three main factors.

Skewed thinking – cognitive distortions

Once your eating disorder has become an indelible habit, it begins to change the way you think and feel about the world. You see the world through the eyes of your disorder. For example, if you are falling behind at work, you may choose to blame this on some subtle change in your body shape or weight, and to exaggerate the problem. We have a model for analysing cognitive distortions, forming part of the therapy known as cognitive therapy. This includes identifying distorted thoughts that men with eating disorders develop. Examples of such distorted thoughts include:

- magnification of problems
- minimisation of successes
- drawing arbitrary inferences (unsupported assumptions) on the basis of nebulous events
- thinking in dichotomous terms (black-and-white thinking)
- personalising issues
- paying selective attention to certain events over others.

I will discuss these in greater detail in Chapter 16.

The anorectic begins to see through anorectic's eyes, the bulimic sees the world in a particular bulimic framework. Men with muscle dysmorphia likewise will judge themselves according to their altered way of thinking. These cognitive distortions alter the whole way you see yourself, your world and your future, like a computer program with a virus. Like anti-virus software, cognitive therapy can profoundly improve the programming, and also ensure you don't pick up another virus.

Relationships

Once you develop an eating disorder, other people's reactions can then subtly perpetuate it. Take the example of Stephen:

Stephen first developed symptoms of bulimia nervosa as a teenager, and on two subsequent occasions dipped into fully fledged anorexia nervosa. On both occasions in which he developed anorexia he required admission to a specialist eating disorder unit.

His parents had been on the brink of divorce for the past five years, and his mother was fighting her own alcohol problems. Stephen had always been extremely close to his mother. On each occasion of his admission to hospital, the marital problems were put on hold and his parents resolved to stay together. Furthermore, mother's alcohol consumption would diminish. Stephen's illness seemed almost to return the family to the happier state he had known as a young lad. In an odd way, his anorexia nervosa helped to hold the family together.

Family therapy proved critical to resolving the situation, helping him form an understanding that his mother's alcohol disorder and his parents' divorce were not his responsibility. It also assisted his family in understanding the impact of their overt behaviour on him.

Family and interpersonal factors are by no means always problematic in body image disorders. But it is not uncommon for people to realise that they need to change the world around them, including relationships, if they are to succeed in changing themselves.

Physiology

Once you have developed a pattern of disordered eating or over-exercise, it can be quite hard to break that pattern. For example, if you exist on a low calorie diet for a long period of time, the satiety signals sent from stomach to brain alter. Very small amounts of foods will make your stomach feel large and bloated, and uncomfortably full. Gaining weight requires consumption of amounts of food that can feel vast, even though in reality they are perfectly appropriate. Your brain has been tricked into adapting to the abnormal circumstances of your eating disorder. Thus someone with anorexia nervosa may need to eat beyond the feeling of fullness. Adaptation to abnormal physiology means you can't always trust your brain to tell you what's good for you.

Summary

It is impossible to provide a comprehensive description of all causes of male body image disorders. There will be many blanks in the above. You will be able to fill in some blanks for yourself. Try it now using Table 7.1. It isn't always necessary to understand all the causes of your body image disorder

Table 7.1 Causes of male body image disorders

	Predisposing factors	Precipitating factors	Perpetuating factors
Physical factors (e.g. genetics and family traits, childhood illnesses)			
Psychological factors (e.g. distorted thinking, personality)			
Social factors (e.g. relationships leaving home for the first time)			

in order to escape from it. Sometimes it is enough simply to address the behaviours and habits that have kept it going. On the other hand, some men with eating disorders require specialist therapy to explore the issues. Formulating your illness in terms of predisposing, precipitating and perpetuating factors is one technique that can help you understand yourself a bit better.

Chapter 8

Compulsive exercise
When does exercise become unhealthy?

Peter's story

Peter trains five times a week with the athletic squad. He wants to be the best, like his dad, and gets worried when he lets his regime slip. He always knows when he is slacking, because his jeans feel a bit tighter, his times start to go down and he has to watch his weight. Sometimes it has been enough to simply knock the weekend beers on the head, but sometimes he has started to skip breakfast before a training session. He is the captain and wants to inspire his team with confidence, so he starts to train for an hour before the proper training session begins.

When he hasn't been eating enough, he knows it has an impact on his performance, and on a couple of occasions he fainted in the changing rooms. His skin has started to suffer, going spotty, and people have told him he looks exhausted. Usually he falls asleep in front of the television when he goes round to see his girlfriend.

He develops an Achilles tendon injury and is advised to rest. He is devastated, feels restless and agitated, as well as guilty. He notices his weight beginning to creep up, so he tries out a run. The pain from his Achilles is terrible, but he learns to take strong painkillers before a run. Every morning he gets out of bed and can hardly walk. His Achilles tendon is tense and sore. He continues to train despite the injury.

Exercise is healthy, only sometimes it isn't. It's not just about the physical effects, but also the compulsion to do it, the guilt when you miss a session and the neglect of other aspects of a well-rounded life. We are surrounded by advertising slogans telling us that it is somehow sexy to go to such extremes, but imagine what it would be like to be Peter's girlfriend. When does healthy exercise become compulsive?

Excess

We live in a world of excess. We are told that obesity is pandemic and will bankrupt the UK health service in the next decade. Regular exercise doesn't just help to maintain a healthy body, it also creates a healthy mind. Studies show that aerobic exercise can help in mild depression. Sportsmen are notable, not to say notorious, for their high self-esteem. Sports psychology teaches us the benefits of positive thinking. The endorphins generated by exercise make us feel more alert and alive, receptive to the world, optimistic and happy. These naturally generated chemicals actually alter our perception of the world. Colour looks brighter, food tastes sharper and emotions are intensified. Sounds like a drug? Well, the body has a clever knack of making sure that its natural chemicals are delivered in a dose and form that only does us good. But even these natural chemicals can be addictive. What are the warning signs?

Cold turkey?

First, exercising for weight loss is always a slippery slope. Exercising for health and fitness is all right, but over-exercising to achieve weight loss can get very addictive. Some people use exercise as a form of pay-off for food consumed at other times. Some people get caught in a vicious cycle of exercise and emaciation. As you have already learnt, at lower weight the body seems to release a primitive foraging behaviour that makes people with anorexia nervosa restless, agitated and physically active. What starts out as a conscious effort to control weight by burning calories becomes an automatic and unconscious activity over which you feel you have no control. Feeling you can't control your level of exercise is the first sign that you have a problem. If you couldn't imagine a week's holiday without working out, running or pumping iron, then you may well have a problem. Rest is an essential component of staying fit, and if you're incapable of it, then your exercise regime is no longer healthy.

Exercising after injury

Exercise is supposed to be healthy, but some athletes exercise well beyond the bounds of health. Peter continued to exercise despite fainting and general physical debilitation, even after he had damaged his Achilles tendon. Some runners are so appalled at missing their evening run that they continue despite major musculoskeletal injuries or even fractures. Rest is an integral part of keeping fit. The body needs activity but it also needs rest. If you feel compelled to exercise despite it causing more harm than good, then you know you have a problem.

Compulsions are physical or mental repetitive behaviours that relieve anxiety and are applied by a set of rigid rules. Normally you know in your heart that your exercise is not really solving the problem, but you cannot resist. Every time you succumb, you feel less anxious. It is this capacity to neutralise anxiety that is so addictive. Since the exercise worked the first time, it will work again. This is what is technically termed a conditioned response and it feeds the cycle of compulsive exercise. For the short-term pay-off of relieving anxiety, you simply postpone the debt. If your fitness routine is less about fitness and more about compulsion, then you know you've got a problem.

Health?

Most people fail to exercise enough. Sixty minutes of moderate exercise every day is hard to achieve. But too much is just as bad as too little. Of course, athletes need to train harder and longer. There has been considerable academic debate about eating disorders in female athletes, who may show virtually all the features of anorexia nervosa except the overt fear of normal body weight.

What really counts is intent. If you find yourself training for a big event, in a training schedule authorised by your trainer, then of course you will be doing more than the average amount of exercise. If after the big event you find you can't stop your training regime, even though there is no goal in mind, because you feel restless and anxious on stopping, or are concerned by weight gain, then undoubtedly you have a problem. There are various 'shades of grey' in between these extremities. Only you can really determine your intent, but a good sign is prioritising fitness over work, studies or friends.

Compulsive exercise checklist

I developed the following checklist as a 'rough and ready' way of identifying that you may have a problem. It isn't definitive and hasn't been tested scientifically in the way that other questionnaires in this book have. Nonetheless, if you answer 'yes' to two or more of these questions then you may have a problem:

* Do you get distressed or guilty if you miss a training session?
* Do you make yourself exercise despite illness or injury?
* Do you put training sessions in front of family or friends?
* Do you exercise as a pay-off for overeating?
* Do you worry about weight gain on rest days?

How to get help

If you think that you are a compulsive exerciser, you should consider using the seven-stage approach described in Part IV of this book. One of the 'behaviour diaries' has been designed for this issue. Consider if your problem goes beyond exercise. Many men with exercise compulsions actually have an eating disorder or muscle dysmorphia, and need to address more than just the exercise itself. If you are in a team, talk to your coach or to a medic attached to your athletic organisation. Many coaches have become very aware of body image disorders in their teams. Some athletic organisations put the health-care profession to shame with their level of knowledge. Don't be afraid of being misunderstood. The stakes are too high. Compulsive exercise, especially when it is combined with an eating disorder, can cause serious and permanent health problems and, in extreme cases, death.

You may wish to consider seeing your family doctor. Particularly for younger men with compulsive exercise problems, there can be problems of body development. Short-term problems of health can become long term.

Change your attitude

Compulsive exercise is an unhappy affair. You never achieve what you set out to achieve. Your best is never good enough. You are using exercise not to improve your muscle efficiency, but to like yourself more. The seven-stage approach in Part IV gives some practical tips for dealing with poor self-esteem and body image.

Start to focus on the positive aspects of exercise. Just as I describe the importance of changing your relationship with food if you have an eating disorder, so should you try and alter your perspective on exercise. For example, periods of rest are crucial in improving muscle efficiency. Give yourself rest days, and remind yourself that this is all part of the training process. Start to think of exercise as one small aspect of 'active relaxation', and think of alternatives. Alternate exercise with other activities. Move away from a puritanical approach to exercise and try to remember back to when it was fun. Choose forms of exercise that are more sociable. Find places to exercise that are more aesthetic – running in a forest as the sun is setting adds a different dimension to training than a laborious slog at the gym. Deliberately stop exercising on the days when you feel most compelled to do so, and then see what it feels like. Try a low impact activity as an alternative to your usual workout.

If your approach to exercise and sport is no longer fun, then do something about it. Having a long break can sometimes be the only way of changing your attitude.

Eating disorders and sport

Sportsmen are at greater risk of eating disorders. This is partly because of the impact of the sport – for example, distance running burns calories and favours an anorectic physique in the short term. Sport can sometimes force you to focus on eating behaviour and weight in a way that may play on your mind. It can also be the case that people with eating disorders are attracted to sport, as a way of expressing their asceticism and masking their problem. Fitness regimes sometimes encourage 'faddy' diets and these can get out of hand. You begin to think of your body as an infinitely malleable machine, there to do your bidding, instead of listening to your body.

If you race in a state of energy depletion at low body mass, then the effects are potentially lethal. Initially you may feel that your performance is unaltered by weight loss, and you may even perceive it to be improved. But eventually you will become ineffective. You may experience a drop in testosterone levels and osteoporosis. At low body mass, sudden exertion can cause the heart to beat irregularly, and this can be fatal.

A coach's guide

The WIPP approach to spotting a problem

If you suspect that one of your team has an eating disorder, then it is unlikely to go away on its own. While changes to diets are common, extreme dietary regimes are rarely helpful. Dietary changes in athletics should not be geared towards weight loss except in a very few cases, and should ideally be supervised by a trained dietician. Any diet should be compiled and monitored very carefully, ideally by an accredited sports dietician. Eating disorders are extremely common in athletes and male athletes may be better at masking their problem than women. Since they may conceal their problem from you, be prepared to look for warning signs, such as those physical effects described in other chapters of this book. Remember WIPP – weight-focused, isolating self, personality change, pushing the goalposts:

- Weight-focused
- Isolation
- Personality change
- Pushing the goalposts.

Weight-focused

Pay particular attention to athletes who have become weight-focused in their training, putting undue emphasis on diet and weight issues. Does he avoid eating with others?

Isolation

Isolating yourself can be a sign that something is wrong. Has his training become solitary?

Personality

Has the person you are training begun to change in personality, becoming uncharacteristically angry, deceitful, or irritable? Is he able to accept praise?

Pushing the goalposts

It may seem to be a sign of strength if the person you are training is setting themselves higher and higher standards, but it could be a manifestation of the illness instead. Is he training beyond his planned schedule, using a very rigid schedule or seeking to continually change that schedule?

Chapter 9

The poisoned chalice

Anabolic steroid abuse

Anabolic steroid abuse is becoming an increasing problem for those of us who treat men with body image disorders. Particularly an issue in boys and men with problems of compulsive exercise and muscle dysmorphia, I have also seen it in a few cases of bulimia nervosa. Steroids are everywhere, and health professionals underestimate their use. Increasingly we hear of famous athletes under suspicion of abusing drugs. But for every one professional athlete seeking enhanced performance, there are many dozen more men seeking the body beautiful. There are no short cuts to the perfect body? Wrong! Imagine a drug will make you bigger and stronger for less effort. Imagine *roids*. While other men are spending hours down the gym honing their bodies, watching their diet, suffering for their art, the steroid abuser can eat all the junk he wants and skip days of training, yet still build muscle bulk.

So why isn't everyone doing it? The fact is that very many actors and sports heroes are reliant on steroids. Steroid abuse has become part of the culture, a hidden part and therefore all the more insidious. And the results are a series of Hollywood role models that would make even Superman feel like Clark Kent. Teenagers watch the movies and are inspired to take short cuts to the impossible body.

Many actresses and models have a percent body fat incompatible with a healthy body, a regular menstrual cycle or a fertile womb. Idealised images of beauty to which young girls are exposed are not consistent with hormonal health. In the same way, the extra-muscular superheroes, male models or actors on the screen present young men with an image of male beauty that cannot be achieved by natural means alone. Men come in all shapes and sizes. When men are inspired to subvert their genetic destiny, there isn't much choice but to follow an unnatural route. For some, this leads to anorexia nervosa and for others to muscle dysmorphia. Body image dissatisfaction stands out as the leading cause of steroid abuse. Although non-prescription steroids are illegal, a hidden industry has arisen to supply the growing demand. Many hundreds of thousands of men are feeding that industry, and only a few of them are professional athletes. Most are men who are simply unhappy with their natural bodies. Clicking on a leading internet health magazines, I follow their links and within two minutes I am instructed how to order illegal steroids via email, how to administer steroids and even how to avoid detection from drug-screening programmes. With such ease of availability, just how widespread is the problem?

An epidemic?

In 1993 a study of American students under the age of 15 found that roughly one in 15 boys had been abusing anabolic steroids. This study, reported in the *New England Journal of Medicine*, confirmed earlier studies that had suggested an epidemic in adolescents and young men. The dearth of comparable studies in Europe suggests that the problem has not been taken seriously, but all the evidence points to a similar epidemic beyond the USA. For instance, the British Medical Association reported that almost half the members of body-building gyms had taken muscle-building drugs, and steroid use was as high as one in eight in some fitness centres. Government agencies are only now waking up to the need for preventative measures.

Facts about anabolic steroids

Just what are they?

Anabolic steroids are hormones similar to testosterone that increase muscle growth and bulk. Occasionally useful for medical purposes such as specific forms of anaemia, they have become drugs of abuse on account of their impact on physical appearance and sports performance. Anabolic literally means growing, and that's just what anabolic steroids do. Testosterone is key to masculine development in puberty, and anabolic steroids mimic the effects of testosterone on growth, body hair and aggressive behaviour.

Who uses them?

In the past, anabolic steroids were abused by professional athletes whose livelihood depended on athletic performance. Increasingly, they are being abused by young men for principally cosmetic reasons: men who hate their bodies; adolescents who want to look bigger, 'sexier' and more powerful. Often they learn to use anabolic steroids from observing their friends, regardless of the cost to their health and well-being. Anabolic steroid abusers come from all walks of life, regardless of social class, race or culture.

What is the language of steroid abuse?

As with all drug subcultures, steroid abuse has generated its own language. Anabolic steroids, or *roids*, are commonly taken by *cycling*, or administering repeated applications of steroids over a fixed time span, with drug free 'holidays' between applications. Cycles generally last for up to 12 weeks. Roids may be *blended* or mixed with a variety of different drugs. Some anabolic steroid abusers will *megadose* by taking huge quantities of drugs. Medically prescribed anabolic steroids are usually administered with a daily dose of around 2 to 3 mg. Anabolic steroid abusers, however, may take a dose one hundred times greater. This may be the result of *plateauing*, whereby a drug dose that was previously effective loses its potency. In medical terms this is known as *tolerance*, recognised as an important factor in development of addictions. Alternatively, steroid users may have a strategy of shotgunning, using anabolic steroids on an ad hoc basis, or *stacking* by combining a wide variety of different anabolic steroids and related substances, such as antidepressants and painkillers.

Having achieved the ultimate goal of *bulking up*, a user may then avoid abrupt withdrawal by gradually reducing the quantity and dose of steroids. Complications of steroid abuse are so well recognised by the users that they have generated their own vocabulary, including *roid rage* to describe the syndrome of uncontainable aggressive behaviour that may decimate the lives of steroid abuses and those around them, and *bitch tits* to describe the growth of breast tissue as a hormonal side effect.

What will steroids due to my body?

Steroids work. It is naive to overlook the efficacy of steroids in building muscle. Steroids increase physical endurance, muscle bulk and strength. In one cycle alone anabolic steroids may increase the user's weight by several pounds, most of which is represented by muscle.

Many of the effects of steroids are obvious and fairly immediate. These include a rapid rise in muscle bulk and acne. But the more worrying effects are well hidden, and these may not be manifest until much later in life. As a result, it is easy for steroid users to dismiss warnings of medical dangers. In an understandable effort to dissuade people from using steroids, some of the medical dangers have been exaggerated. For example, there have been a few cases of liver cancer caused by megadosing on steroids, but the average steroid user is unlikely to know anyone suffering from this effect. As a result of these true but exaggerated warnings, there is a real danger that all the warnings will be dismissed as sanctimonious bunkum. Table 9.1 attempts to lay out complications in terms of long-term outcomes and reversibility.

There are two limitations in persuading men to avoid steroids by such information. First, many of the serious physical effects take time to develop, and most of us make decisions in life based on short-term, not long-term, goals. Second, some but not all of the serious effects are rare. If you start to take steroids and find you haven't gone bald, you begin to doubt the medical advice.

Table 9.1 Complications from long-term use of steroids

Body system	Side effect	Long-term effect
Cardiovascular	Increased fats and cholesterol levels	Reversible on steroid cessation
	Raised blood pressure	Probably reversible on steroid cessation
	'Furring' of the heart and its arteries (arteriosclerosis)	Irreversible
Liver	Raised levels of liver enzymes (as in excessive alcohol use)	Reversible on steroid cessation
	Jaundice	Reversible on steroid cessation
	Liver cancer	Irreversible
Muscles and skeleton	In adolescents only: premature cessation of bone growth (epiphyseal closure) with consequent stunting	Irreversible
	Tendon damage	Long-term effects not yet established
Hormones	Changes in glucose tolerance (as in diabetes)	Reversible on steroid cessation
	Lowering in essential sex hormones (FSH, LH)	Reversible on steroid cessation
Skin	Acne vulgaris	Yes (except acne scarring)
Reproductive system	Shrinkage of the testicles	Partially reversible
	Growth of breast tissues (bitch tits)	Long-term effects not yet established
	Reduced sperm count	Probably reversible on steroid cessation
	Changes in sex drive (raised or lowered according to pattern of cycling)	Reversible on steroid cessation
	Male pattern baldness	Irreversible
	Infertility	Probably reversible on steroid cessation

Greg is in his late twenties and attends a gym in London. He has been using steroids for the past four years. His use has included megadosing and stacking:

> In the first six months my weight went up 50 or 60 pounds. I could bench-press much more than ever. I looked pumped up. All those things I'd been warned about, they either never happened or they didn't seem to matter.
>
> I got a few spots on my chin and on my chest, but nothing I couldn't handle. My balls got a bit smaller, but that reversed when I stopped my regime. I knew some guys who lost a bit of hair, but that never happened to me. Maybe my breasts grew a bit, but it was difficult to tell 'cos my pecs were so big anyway. And that's about it.
>
> I'd been expecting liver failure, cancers, impotence, but it wasn't like that at all. I gave up listening to all the scare stories. They just didn't make any sense.

His statement is characteristic of many steroid users. It exemplifies the dangers of exaggerating the warnings and the difficulties of achieving the right balance between true advice and scaremongering. The fact is that steroids can produce serious side effects, but many people escape them. The emotional effects of steroids can be far more immediate and serious.

What will steroids do to my mind?

Steroids can profoundly alter the emotions and personalities of users. Unlike many of the physical side effects outlined above, the psychological effects are common and well recognised among users. The degree of these effects is often missed by the user themselves. How easy is it to recognise that you have changed as a person or are causing distress to those you love? But no one doubts that steroids have the potential to poison the brain, a poisoned chalice. Their effects range from direct impact of the drug on the brain to the consequences of steroid dependence and withdrawal.

Direct psychiatric effects of steroids

In 2000, a male nurse working in the UK carried out a frenzied stabbing attack on a colleague who subsequently died of his injuries. It transpired that he had started to show signs of change in another hospital. In a separate incident he had slapped a female member of staff, as part of an apparent pattern of hostility shown towards his colleagues. He attacked his final victim in front of patients in a hospital, approaching him from behind and slashing him in a 'ferocious onslaught'. In the course of his trial it emerged that he had been abusing steroids for years as part of his body-building hobby. It appeared that he had suffered from paranoid delusions and he admitted manslaughter on the grounds of diminished responsibility. This case comes from a long line of reported cases of steroid-induced psychiatric symptoms, most occurring in the USA. Recently the same trend began to emerge in Europe.

The direct psychiatric effects vary from irritability and unusually aggressive behaviour to frank paranoid delusions and exaggeration of pre-existing personality traits. In one 1994 study, reported in *Archives of General Psychiatry*, a quarter of steroid users were found to be suffering from symptoms suggesting a major mood disorder, including mania and major depression. In 1996 two violent murders in Sydney Australia were reported in a medical journal in which anabolic steroids were the cause. In another study published in *Annals of Clinical Psychiatry*, Choi and Pope found that partners of men using anabolic steroids were at a significantly elevated risk of serious injury, including physical violence and abuse as well as verbal aggression.

Not simply of risk to others, anabolic steroid users have an elevated risk of injury and even death as a result of their own impulsiveness and dis-inhibited behaviour. A study in the Karolinska Institute in Sweden found that the vast majority of unexpected deaths amongst users of anabolic steroids were the result of homicides, suicides and poisonings related to impulsive and disinhibited behaviour. The behaviour included violent rages and mood swings, as well as depressive symptoms.

Clearly these descriptions lie at the extreme end of psychiatric problems associated with steroid abuse. But think what this means for the majority of steroid abusers who never make it into the papers. The concept of *roid rage* is now well established and characterised by explosive aggressive behaviour. But so subtle are the effects of steroids on the mind that acts of aggression may arise slowly and with foresight, rather than necessarily representing a provoked response in a crisis.

Peter's story

Peter was a policeman and also worked as a volunteer youth worker in his local community. He was respected and liked in equal measure. However, he had started to use steroids as his athletic prowess declined with age. Verbal aggression and jealousy towards his girlfriend had caused the ending of their long-lasting relationship. His work colleagues found him increasingly insuffer-able. He was only half-aware of this and in some ways had been relieved to split with his girlfriend 'because she was doing my head in'.

Then one day, sitting peacefully at home, he exploded at the noise from workmen outside his house. Leaping to his feet, he ran into the street shouting, his formidable presence striking terror into the hearts of the bemused road diggers. Grabbing one by the scruff of his neck, he shouted in his face. Later, he recalled the exhilaration of feeling so powerful, relishing the opportunity of a fight.

Luckily he still had some insight into his own behaviour, partly realising how disproportionate his reactions had been. He managed to calm himself down and even apologise in an act of supreme self-mastery, before returning to his house. In a sense, this crisis 'brought me to my senses', causing him to seek medical and psychological treatment.

Anecdotes are backed up by hard scientific fact. Many studies show that megadoses of anabolic steroids cause experimental subjects to display personality changes including extreme irritability and explosive aggression, an exaggerated sense of one's own powers and abilities, and 'territorial behaviour'. Contrary to the suggestion that men who use steroids in the context of body building are already somehow psychologically vulnerable, this phenomenon has even been found in men who have no history of going to the gym, in controlled experimental conditions. It's not just a few 'odd-balls' who go crazy on steroids, it seems to be quite usual. Just as men may react very differently in response to alcohol or show differing reactions according to their current mood and social circumstances, so the effects of steroids on the brain can be subtle and difficult to anticipate. Nonetheless the problem is immense and can lead to tragic consequences.

Steroid dependence

It is increasingly recognised that steroids can be drugs of addiction. I have already remarked on the plateauing effect of steroids in some users, in which previously potent doses no longer work, leading the user to inject higher and higher doses to achieve the same effect. But this is only part of the cycle of addiction in steroids.

While taking steroids, the body's own natural ability to produce testosterone is suppressed. This explains why the genitals begin to shrink. So, when anabolic steroids are stopped, there is a lag-period while the body desperately begins to resume its previous functioning. During this period many men will present as lethargic, lacking in energy and motivation, with sleep disturbance, a loss of appetitive drive, including loss of hunger for food and sexual desire. In some cases this produces a fully fledged major depressive illness which may even result in suicide attempts.

In one study Malone and colleagues found that as many as one in 15 steroid users had attempted suicide at one stage or another during steroid withdrawal. A combination of chemical effects of steroid cessation, the body's own reaction to the withdrawal of the hormones and the psychological impact of loss of muscle bulk create a complex syndrome of addiction. This is certainly not in the same league as heroin or nicotine

Table 9.2 Effects of steroids

Mental effect	Symptoms	Probability
Mania	Feelings of elation and omnipotence	Rare
Mood swings	Irritability, impulsivity	Common
Violence and aggression		Common
Depression	Loss of pleasure, sleep disturbance, changes in appetite, thoughts of suicide	Common
Impairment of judgement	Lack of forward planning, unable to 'see the wood for the trees'	Common
Delusions	Firmly held beliefs that people are plotting against you or disparaging you	Rare
Paranoid jealousy	Firmly held beliefs that your partner is unfaithful, seeing the 'proof' in trivial things	Rare

addiction, in terms of physical dependence, but it is sufficient to result in suffering and distress, driving the sufferer either back into the cycle of steroid abuse or even so far as to attempt suicide.

How do I stop taking anabolic steroids?

Step one: recognise the problem

First, you must recognise that you have a problem. Most people taking anabolic steroids fall at this hurdle. They see their steroid abuse as a lifestyle choice, unconnected with illicit drug use. Humans have an infinite capacity to con themselves into justifying their actions. Anabolic steroid abusers can be as deluded about their body size as people with anorexia nervosa, albeit in the opposite direction. But any anabolic steroid *use* is *abuse*. Anyone taking anabolic steroids has a problem. Forget for the moment that anabolic steroids are illegal. Forget that selling anabolic steroids is a criminal offence. Indeed, this may only increase their glamour for some users, for whom the risk taking simply makes steroids seem more 'hard core'. Instead, ask yourself whether the body shape you have achieved through anabolic steroids is sustainable? Now imagine yourself in thirty years time. You're standing alone in the bathroom. You're looking at your body in the mirror. Will you still be using steroids? If so, what harm could you have done to that body? What will it really look like? If not, how can you find a fitness regime you can maintain and sustain for the next 30 years? How can you be 'fit for life' if your current body shape is so artificially achieved? Or do you want to live fast, die younger and make a muscular corpse?

Step two: make an inventory

Go back to Tables 9.1 and 9.2 on the physical and psychological effects. How many of these complications might apply to you? Write them down. At first you may be reluctant to think that you become more aggressive since taking roids. Perhaps you've just become more self-confident now you've got the body you've always wanted? But entertain the possibility for a second. Could you have changed as a person? Even if you don't think so, have your relationships with other people changed? Now imagine it's your partner or friend describing you, maybe a family member, maybe someone you respect. Listen to their voice. How would they describe the changes in you? List the ways you may have changed.

Are there other hidden costs to your steroid use? How much money have you been spending? Have you shared a needle to inject steroids? Have you ever used a needle that wasn't freshly packed? Do you think you should be tested for HIV or hepatitis? Consider telling someone. Or are you reluctant to confide? Ask yourself why.

Chapter 10

Physical health and body image disorders

Having a body image disorder is frightening stuff. As a doctor, the last thing I want is to add to your fears. Nonetheless, there is no doubt that body image disorders carry a physical risk. It is important you know all the facts. Any man reading *The Invisible Man* will already have awareness of some of the effects on the body, though you may choose to disregard them. It is not my intention to frighten you into seeking treatment, but rather to give you enough information to weigh up the risks.

Mortality

'No man is an Island, entire of it self'

Eating disorders do carry a risk of death. While bulimia nervosa and muscle dysmorphia are not without risk, anorexia nervosa is the most lethal. Indeed, it is the most lethal of all mental conditions. The studies that have been carried out for the longest periods of time have concluded that the risk of death is in the order of one in five for those who have not received treatment. This falls to around one in 20 for people who receive treatment. Doctors can try to minimise the risk of death, but we do not always win. It is critical to find a clinician who can manage the physical as well as psychological complications.

Some people with anorexia nervosa are very frightened of death but may hold distorted beliefs around risks. Pro-anorexia websites have suggested that anorexia nervosa is healthy and life-prolonging. People with eating disorders soak up distorted information like sponges, by way of false reassurance, but this is nonsense. I have been part of a group looking at how to predict risk of death in eating disorders. As such, I have been exposed to the heart-breaking narratives of families and friends who have lost loved ones to anorexia nervosa. There is no doubt that many people die needlessly, often in the prime of their lives.

For others, the fear of death is simply not there at all. The thought of dying by starvation becomes attractive in the midst of existential despair.

Some believe that dying will relieve their families of a burden. In reality, the death of a loved one haunts families and friends. The impact passes down generations. It can be like dropping a small pebble through the still surface of a lake. The ripples expand and expand. The impact goes on and on. It is difficult to escape this responsibility. You may believe you live in splendid isolation from others, but we are all interconnected. John Donne, the metaphysical Renaissance poet, eloquently summed this up:

> No man is an Island, entire of it self; . . . any man's death diminishes me, because I am involved in Mankind; And therefore never send to know for whom the bell tolls; it tolls for thee.
>
> (Meditation XVII, John Donne, 1624)

Thankfully, most men with body image problems or eating disorders do not die, but the physical effects are severe and disabling.

Effects of exercise

Over-exercising is particularly common in men with eating disorders. Modest exercise can be helpful, particularly as part of a strategy of 'active relaxation'. But for many men with body image disorders, exercise is intrinsically tethered to their underlying illness. Initially, exercise can be driven by a conscious desire to change body shape and weight. But later it becomes a habit, over which the sufferer has little control or awareness. At very low weights, the effects of exercise are amplified. Muscle injuries become more common, and repair of muscle damage takes longer in a state of malnutrition. Osteoporosis (thinning bones) is extremely common, and so the athlete becomes more vulnerable to stress fractures. Emaciation alters the function of the heart and, when this is coupled with exercise, there is a risk of the heart beating irregularly, causing a heart attack. Exercise places demands on stored energy supplies in the body. Where these have already been exhausted through starvation, exercise speeds you into low blood sugar levels, causing loss of concentration, confusion and even a coma. It can be very hard to judge for yourself when this state arrives. (Exercise is also discussed in greater detail in Chapter 8.)

Emaciation

Where an eating disorder occurs before or during puberty, bones will fail to develop and growth may be stunted. Puberty itself can be postponed, and this can have a lasting effect on how you develop as a man, including development of primary and secondary sexual characteristics. As mentioned above, there is an increased risk of osteoporosis. Osteoporosis is a condition of thinning bones, normally associated with women after the menopause. It can be due to a combination of altered hormones or a lack of essential vitamins and minerals. While hormonal factors appear to be predominant, unfortunately recent studies suggest that giving artificial hormones does not appear very beneficial. We do not have a good solution for men with osteoporosis, although it is common to prescribe hormones and certain vitamins. On a positive note, we believe that many men who develop osteoporosis as a result of anorexia nervosa will be able to recover their bone density when they regain their weight. Weight gain is the only effective solution.

The heart and circulation are affected by emaciation. It is common to develop a slow pulse rate and blood pressure, so your heart no longer works effectively as a pump. In milder cases, there can be poor circulation. Hands may appear cold and blue, and there is a risk of hypothermia. In more serious cases, the heart may work irregularly, fluid builds up in your lungs and other tissues (heart failure), and heart muscle itself may start to break down.

Many men with eating disorders complain of a disturbance of sleep. Sometimes this is put down to the worry and stress of the condition, but we now know that starvation itself produces sleep disturbance. One of the reasons for sleep is to make use of food reserves appropriated during waking hours. Where there has been little or no calorie consumption, sleep loses much of its purpose, which is why many men with eating disorders complain of waking frequently in the night. Sleep has lost its biological purpose.

Some patients in a state of relative or absolute starvation complain of changes in their skin. For example, in 1999 we published research in the *British Journal of Dermatology* demonstrating that extreme low weight causes pruritus, or an unpleasant itching sensation, which then improves as you gain weight. Itching on thin, damaged skin can produce marks and scars called scratch prurigo. Some men grow a fine, downy type of hair on their bodies called Lanugo. All these factors are distressing in themselves, but also can enhance the body image disturbance you are experiencing.

At low weight your hormones change profoundly, and become more like those of a young boy than a man. Testosterone levels go down and, as a result, there is a loss of sex drive. For some men with anorexia nervosa this can be experienced as rather a relief. But we know that a fifth of men with anorexia nervosa experience gender identity disturbance (discussed in Chapter 7), and in part this may be due to the physical impact of starvation on your hormones. It is worth bearing in mind that recovery from emaciation has the reverse effect. Some people have compared it to re-experiencing puberty at both a physical and psychological level. The physical and the psychological effects are deeply entwined, such that it can be fruitless to try and disentangle them. Effective treatments require clinicians with the skills to manage both aspects synchronously.

Chronic starvation eventually alters the way that your gut works. Your stomach learns to perceive quite small amounts of food as being vast, and this can be a barrier to gaining weight, as you will need to eat through the experience of being 'stuffed' in order to receive sufficient calories to gain weight. Your sense of your stomach being full or empty is not really based on its contents, but how the brain perceives things. A chronic state of starvation means that your brain loses touch with reality. Your gut is actually a very complex organ, filled with nerves and chemical signals. The 'waves of contraction' (peristalsis) that your gut would normally experience in healthy digestion of food can be temporarily altered. Contraction of the gut can slow down, and it is common to experience constipation, or a feeling of bloating, especially when you have been using laxatives in the past. Sometimes you may need to endure these sensations while your gut relearns to be healthy.

Poor nutrition affects blood cells. Loss of red blood cells can cause anaemia, making some men feel chronically tired and lethargic. Loss of white blood cells can cause us to be more at risk of coughs and colds. At very low weight, a lack of protein in the bloodstream can paradoxically make the body swell up. If you have seen images of starving children in Third World countries in the media, you will have seen this effect in their distended tummies. In anorexia nervosa it is more common to see the swelling in the legs.

When the body runs out of stored energy reserves, it begins instead to break down muscle. As a result, you may find that the muscles, not only of your arms and legs, but also buttocks and shoulders, begin to shrink. This becomes an important sign for doctors to observe. At the point where a patient is unable to rise unaided from a sitting position, muscle bulk has fallen to a level suggesting the need to be admitted to hospital. For some patients, the effects of starvation on the circulation will cause damage to organs, particularly the heart and the kidneys. Some patients develop kidney failure whilst others experience damage to the heart muscle. A thorough examination of all these organs should be carried out routinely by whoever treats you.

Purging

Many men with bulimia nervosa and anorexia nervosa will purge using vomiting, laxatives or diuretics. All of these carry health risks. The vomiting affects the teeth, causing erosion of enamel. Many patients with bulimia and anorexia are so embarrassed by the state of their teeth that they avoid seeing their dentist. The pattern of enamel erosion is characteristic.

Vomiting makes the salivary glands swell, as if you have mumps. For many patients the effect of this on body image can be quite disturbing. Chronic vomiting can affect the gut, leading to pains in the tummy and sometimes even vomiting blood. The pattern of vomiting becomes a learnt habit. What used to be a conscious effort becomes an easy reflex, which is hard to stop.

The effects of purging are profound on the blood chemistry of the body. Low levels of certain essential blood salts, including potassium, will alter the way that the heart and kidneys work. This can result in an irregular heart and even heart attacks, as well as kidney failure. Whilst thankfully this is only a problem in a minority of patients, most patients who purge will experience apathy, loss of concentration, headaches and a profound fatigue. Where people have been using laxatives over a long period, the gut adapts to the overstimulation and stops working. Whilst rare, paralysis of the gut becomes a surgical emergency. More common is bloating and constipation, or sometimes bleeding from your back passage. The good news is that most of these symptoms stop when your behaviours improve.

Abuse of tablets

Some men with eating disorders misuse anabolic steroids. Steroids do increase physical endurance, muscle bulk and strength. The physical problems associated with anabolic steroids have been described in Chapter 9.

Some people with eating disorders will take stimulant drugs, including diet pills, amphetamines and cocaine, simply in order to control their weight. Others will get hold of water tablets (diuretics). The stimulant pills can have a profound effect on your mood. They make people edgy, irritable, agitated, suspicious and sometimes downright paranoid. Sleep is affected. In the longer term they can cause permanent damage to the heart and circulation. Many people who misuse stimulant drugs will experience epileptic fits. Water tablets simply strip the body of water and related essential salts. This causes the same sort of damage as that described in relation to vomiting. Of course, the impact on weight and shape is non-existent. The loss of water is immediately reversed as soon as you have a drink. The motive to take diuretics is more psychological.

What tests may your physician carry out?

If you consult your physician with an eating disorder, it is common for your blood chemistry to be checked. We particularly look at levels of a salt known as *potassium*. If these potassium levels have fallen into the danger zone, your doctor may become concerned about the effect that this may have on your heart and on your muscles.

Sometimes levels of *sodium* are also affected, and in extreme circumstances this may result in fits and faints. Levels of *bicarbonate* can rise as a result of these effects, and cause the bloodstream to become more alkaline. It is also usual to check levels of *calcium*, *magnesium* and *phosphate*, which should be monitored not only when you are ill, but also when you are recovering. It would be normal for your doctor to manage the situation by getting you to change your habits, for example, by reducing your vomiting. Unless there is a dire emergency, it is best to gradually correct the fault in blood chemistry by slowly changing your habits, and letting your body adjust accordingly. However, in extreme circumstances you may be prescribed various supplements, and even admitted to hospital.

It is usual to look at your blood count to see what effect your eating disorder has had on red blood cells, white blood cells and platelets. This gives us an indication of the working of your bone marrow, as well as anaemia. Again, it is usual to address this, simply by helping the patient to gain weight, but occasionally it is necessary to take additional iron or vitamins and, in extreme circumstances, some patients receive blood transfusions.

It is routine to check the function of the liver and kidneys. Severe starvation can cause the liver to sustain some damage, and this is apparent in blood tests. Furthermore, the liver is the organ of the body most intimately involved in making use of your food consumed, and so it gives an indication of the severity of the anorexia nervosa. We have already mentioned how starvation can cause kidney failure, so it is important for your doctor to check the function of your kidneys through a simple blood test, as well as testing for your blood sugar level.

Sometimes we measure bone density by a special type of scan. This allows us to evaluate if a patient is suffering from thinning bones (osteoporosis). As mentioned above, we do not have a clear strategy for treating osteoporosis. This appears to depend on both hormones and also on calcium and vitamin D intake. However, giving patients exogenous hormones or prescribing calcium and vitamin D do not appear to be very effective strategies. The best remedy is through weight gain, and it may be helpful to consume foods rich in calcium.

Long-term effects

Most of the problems described above will be reversed if you get better. Where the illness has affected you at a critical time in development, such as puberty, there can be lasting effects, including stunting of growth and poorly developed 'secondary sexual characteristics'. Typically, recovery will cause your reproductive hormones to work again, and your sex drive will recover. For some people with eating disorders, this can actually be quite a disturbing process, akin to re-experiencing puberty, both physically and psychologically.

Your bones may recover, but some people will already have experienced fractures in their spines and this can cause the back to be curved and height diminished. Unfortunately, a minority of people with osteoporosis do not recover bone density, even when they regain weight.

Generally, effects of starvation and related behaviours on the heart will be reversed after weight gain. However, occasionally some patients will already have experienced such damage, including heart attacks, which may not have been previously detected, and these effects may persist. It is therefore normal for your doctor to carry out a tracing of your heart activity, known as an ECG. Certain changes in the ECG can be used by doctors to judge if someone is at imminent risk of their heart beating erratically. Your doctor will be skilled in this.

Many men with eating disorders do suffer chronic problems with their bowels even after recovery, and there appears to be a link between chronic irritable bowel symptoms and past eating disorder. Sometimes this is obviously the result of many years of misusing laxatives, but sometimes the cause is unknown.

Summary

Eating disorders have a profound effect on the body as well as the mind. Most of these effects can be reversed with treatment. Most of the effects require expert monitoring and testing. For the patient with anorexia nervosa, weight gain will reverse nearly all of the physical complications. For patients with bulimia nervosa, giving up bingeing and related behaviours will have a rapid effect on feelings of physical vitality. A great deal more research is required on the effects of eating disorders on the body. In the meantime, being aware of those effects can be a source of motivation to recover. In describing the physical problems associated with eating disorders, I am not trying to scare you into such a recovery, but to give you clear facts in order that you make up your own mind.

Chapter 11

Mental health and body image disorders

When you first begin to develop a body image disorder, it is often one of many niggling problems in the back of your mind. However, it will start to loom larger and larger on your horizon, until it becomes the niggling problem, your constant preoccupation. Your thinking about body image can become so deeply ingrained that it is difficult to think about anything else at all. This can have an impact on your hobbies, friendships and work. You may begin to define yourself purely in terms of how you think and feel about your body and its shape.

At the centre of body image disorders is a distortion of perspective, and particularly the emphasis placed on body shape. For the person with low weight anorexia nervosa, there is a complete terror of gaining weight, or becoming fat, even though you are underweight. The same psychological sense of body image disparagement is present in bulimia nervosa and binge eating, but with a sense of dietary chaos. For people with muscle dysmorphia, the mind becomes convinced that you are scrawnier than you really are. This has been termed reverse anorexia, but in reality it stems from the same core body image disparagement. Men with body image problems are far more likely to focus on issues of shape than on absolutes of weight. This is very similar in anorexia nervosa, bulimia and muscle dysmorphia. That is why I argued in an editorial in the *Lancet* in 2000 that all three conditions should be classed together.

Many doctors are used to expecting patients with eating disorders to have a preoccupation with body weight; perhaps a detailed knowledge of the fluctuations in their weight, or an aversion to being weighed, with a clear goal of weight loss. However, men with eating disorders will be much more likely to alter their behaviours according to how their different body parts appear and how their shape is delineated, rather than a tendency to weigh themselves. This is one of several reasons why men with eating disorders tend to be under diagnosed by doctors.

It can be useful to think of the mental impact of body image disorders in terms of the core and the non-core effects. By 'core' I mean the issues already described above, intrinsic to the disorder. By 'non-core', I mean the secondary effects of the disorder, for example, simply the effect of physical behaviours such as starvation on the mind. To understand the latter, we are able to draw on a wide number of studies that have been carried out on people who do not have eating disorders, but are otherwise malnourished.

The core psychopathology

Body image disorders were first characterised in 1689. From that time onwards, different commentators have speculated on the nature of the core psychopathology involved. The earlier doctors construed eating disorders in terms of a wasting away of the nerves; for example Morton described it as a 'nervous consumption' and Whytt as a 'nervous atrophy'. Only in the twentieth century did it become apparent that the driving force was a desire to alter body shape. For example, Hilde Bruch characterised anorexia nervosa as a 'relentless pursuit of thinness'. We would now tend to turn this on its head and consider anorexia nervosa as being principally driven by an absolute dread of fatness, regarded as a very intrusive and overvalued idea that you simply cannot shift from your head.

Associated with this is a distortion of body image. Classically, this is seen as involving a visual body size over-estimation in anorexia nervosa and usually bulimia, or under-estimation in muscle dysmorphia, in which patients visualise themselves as being far different to objective reality. However, from my clinical practice I think this can sometimes miss the point. It is more about the moral imperative placed on changes in body image than simply a visual misperception. Many patients do not have distortions in their perceptual approach to their bodies. It is rather how they evaluate themselves, their attitudes and beliefs. The inability to control your body shape is seen as a sign of moral weakness, and people begin to talk of themselves as 'good' or 'bad', 'greedy', or even 'wicked'.

This way of thinking has been termed 'ego-syntonic'. This rather technical term means that the disorder is not experienced as a problem in itself, but rather as a solution to a problem. On that basis, you will not go battering down the door of your doctor seeking treatment. Rather, you are contented within your illness and can feel disturbed by the well-meaning interventions of friends and family. Professor Arthur Crisp, a leading expert in the field, has suggested that body image disorders are actually 'adaptive'. In other words, at times of great insecurity, your body image disorder is a means of controlling yourself and the world around you, however unsustainable that might be. It is only by being able to explore such issues of control in therapy that you can truly make the decision to get better.

Eventually the self-esteem of someone with a body image disorder becomes entirely dependent upon control of body shape. You may get a first class honours degree, win the cross-country running championship or become a professor of business studies, but nothing counts for anything if you have gained a kilogram in weight or missed a work-out at the gym.

The one thing we do not see in anorexia nervosa is 'anorexia'. Anorexia is a medical term meaning 'loss of appetite'. In anorexia nervosa, appetite is usually preserved but subverted. Of course, after chronic malnutrition, one's sense of appetite becomes quite disordered. But initially there are no problems with appetite, and exploring these issues helps doctors differentiate anorexia nervosa from other emotional causes of weight loss such as depression, where appetite is generally lost. Men with eating disorders are attempting to conquer their appetite, not to lose it.

The non-core psychopathology

Some aspects of body image disorders are the result of secondary nutrition rather than the primary emotional state. A few decades ago, we carried out experiments on medical students. Some of those studies involved depriving them of food, but keeping them adequately hydrated. There have also been studies on nutrition, thoughts and feelings on large societies that have suffered from famine. By combining our knowledge of temporary starvation with our knowledge of effects of famine, we can now conclude that some aspects of body image disorders result from malnutrition, rather than being primary in their own right. These tend to get better more quickly as the nutritional problems are treated, whereas the thought processes can linger on and require more subtle therapies.

Melancholia and depression are very commonly a result of malnutrition. A minority of men with body image disorders have started off with a primary depressive illness requiring treatment in its own right, and the body image disorder is a psychological defence against that depression. Such people need proper treatment of their depressive illness as well as their eating disorder. However, some men with body image disorders are misdiagnosed as having depression and treated with antidepressants where psychotherapy and nutritional rehabilitation may be preferable. Generally speaking, depression and low mood tend to improve as you gain in weight, and therefore weight gain is a treatment of choice.

Many men with body image disorders withdraw from society. Of course, this can be part of the disorder itself, or maybe a direct or indirect consequence of the illness. We can see exaggeration of the pre-existing personality traits. For example, someone who is introverted or has low self-esteem may become an even paler shadow of their former self. However, apparent changes in personality can be quite inconsistent with past temperament. A happy, loving, honest son may become angry, impulsive, 'manipulative', or deceitful. In extreme cases, I have known patients steal food from shops, whereas in the past they would regard such dishonesty as abhorrent.

Indeed, eating disorders have been successfully cited as a legal defence, in terms of this impact on personality.

Eventually body image manipulation becomes the sole source of identity in a rather fragile ego. This can permit control over the world around you. For example, if you feel trapped in a difficult relationship with a partner, or parent, yet dare not put your feelings into words, you dissipate those feelings through your disordered eating. Again, here I would emphasise the useful model of a body image disorder as adaptive and a 'solution to a problem'.

Poor nutrition often results in a loss of sexual libido. We have a clear understanding of this in biological terms. Your brain has evolved to respond differently to times of famine and times of feast. Thus parts of the brain called the hypothalamus and pituitary have developed to be extremely sensitive to nutrition. One element of this is for poor nutrition to reduce your sex drive and reduce levels of hormones such as testosterone. For some men with body image disorders, this provides a blessed relief and can even be an aspect of the illness. Of course, for others this loss of libido is upsetting and disturbing.

Eventually malnutrition affects the way you think, at quite a basic level. You may find you simply cannot pay attention to things. This may affect your ability to remember things, or may render you unsafe to drive a car. Many people with eating disorders are highly intelligent, but you might discover that you have difficulty in completing even basic tasks, such as remembering someone's telephone number. This can actually affect your ability to reason, or what is technically termed 'mental capacity'. You may simply not understand what doctors are saying to you or, despite understanding, you may not be able to remember it for long enough in order to reach a decision.

It is not possible to provide an exhaustive list of all the ways in which malnutrition can impact on mood and personality. It can be extremely difficult to tease apart the various factors, and separate the chickens from the eggs. But the take-home message is that malnutrition profoundly alters our thoughts, feelings and behaviours. More importantly, improving your nutritional status can have rapid impact on a host of issues, including low mood, poor sleep and inadequate concentration.

Behaviours

Body image disorders translate 'ways of thinking' into 'ways of doing'. A repertoire of behaviours emerges around the disorder. Many of these have been discussed in other chapters. Once you are completely trapped by your illness, it can be difficult to disentangle all these various behaviours. The obvious behaviour is dietary restriction. Dietary trends in people with eating disorders often mirror dietary trends espoused in the media. This can vary from avoidance of sugar and carbohydrate to extreme veganism. Of course, vegetarianism and veganism are entirely appropriate ethical stances.

Odd eating behaviours might emerge. This might include the secret disposal of food, cutting food up into smaller portions, use of unusual utensils for eating, extremely slow eating patterns, refusal to eat with other people, eating only at night, and 'salinophagia' or the spoiling of food with salt.

The use of exercise in body image disorders begins as conscious, hidden and obsessional. You may begin your exercise regime in the middle of the night, so that your family do not realise. It may involve the use of pay-offs: 'If I am going to have to eat Sunday roast, at least I can do one hundred press-ups afterwards.'

Later, aspects of over-activity are secondary to malnutrition, representing an unconscious foraging behaviour. There is a persistent sense of inner restlessness that can be quite distressing. You may find your sleep becomes disturbed, with difficulty in getting off to sleep, or with frequent waking in the night. Again, this appears to be a consequence of nutrition. One of the tasks of sleep is to make use of food resources gathered during the day. If nothing has been gathered, then your body becomes restless and your ability to sleep is reduced, as your brain instructs you to be hunting and gathering. The senses of restlessness and sleep disturbance seem to represent this primitive hunter-gatherer behaviour.

Another effect of poor nutrition is to make the brain preoccupied with aspects of food, and creates behaviours such as calorie counting, cooking or weighing food. Paradoxically you may begin to read recipe books, or go shopping for food and enjoy preparing food for other people without actually eating it yourself. This can be tethered to other obsessional ruminations and rituals, not necessarily related to eating disorders. Many people with eating disorders do show these additional obsessional traits, such as cleaning or checking rituals.

So far we have discussed behaviours relating to the burning of calories, either by calorie restriction or by over-exercise. However, there are arrays of purging behaviours that often accompany body image disorders. People induce vomiting by various methods. Some men recall the discovery of purging with great alacrity. 'At last, I can eat whatever I want and get away with it!' Of course, the reality is very different, but purging temporarily alleviates extreme distress around body image, so becomes a hugely attractive way of conning yourself into thinking you have control. People take slimming pills or laxatives to control their body weight. In reality laxatives simply generate water loss, but from a psychological point of view there is a strong sense of being cleansed. In the same way, men may misuse enemas or diuretics. Diuretic misuse is common in muscle dysmorphia and can be combined with anabolic steroid abuse.

Some men take stimulant drugs such as amphetamines and cocaine purely for the effects on weight and not to 'get high'. In our research we have shown body image disorders as a common reason for persistent cigarette smoking. Smoking is an appetite suppressant, and stopping smoking is often associated with weight gain. It is easy to understand why national smoking cessation programmes have failed those smokers who have underlying body image problems. Beneath all these purging behaviours is the sense of absolute dietary chaos. In physical terms, you swing from extremes of fullness to extremes of starvation. In psychological terms this is mirrored by a vicious cycle of self-loathing and relief.

Just as with starvation, purging can be 'adaptive' – the instant relief of intense disgust becomes extremely attractive. In simple terms, anything making you feel instantly good is likely to get its claws into you and become compulsive. All the effective treatments of body image disorders involve the unfortunate necessity of sitting there 'feeling bloody awful' until that feeling goes away, rather than resorting to behaviours that give instant gratification but perpetuate the problem. For this reason, some people regard eating disorders as a form of 'addiction'.

Are body image disorders addictions?

The argument over addictions and body image disorders rages in academic circles, and ultimately this can be quite sterile for people who suffer body image disorders. The 'addiction model' argues that certain people are at risk of becoming quite dependent on certain types of foods, and this resembles a chemical dependence. On that basis, the argument is that they should abstain from these foods and that the treatments of eating disorders should be similar to the treatments used in various addictions.

I have rarely found this a helpful approach. Addiction does indeed explain some aspects of body image disorders, and certain treatments used in addictions, such as motivational enhancement therapy and the 12-steps approach, can be very useful in body image disorders. But they just scratch the surface. A notion of body image disorders as addictions can explain the 'whats' but not the 'whys' or 'wherefores'. People who are physically addicted to chemicals show tolerance, dependence and withdrawal. Tolerance means that you will need increasing doses of the same chemical in order to produce the same effect. There is no evidence that this applies in eating disorders. There is no evidence of physical dependence on foods in eating disorders. Some people with bulimia nervosa may have a craving for chocolate, but this is very different to going 'cold turkey', when you stop taking heroin. Another argument has been that certain people are more susceptible to carbohydrate cravings and that this has a chemical basis. It is certainly true that carbohydrates have an impact on the brain chemistry. The intake of carbohydrates can cause an increase in a brain chemical called serotonin, which is implicated in mood. There is evidence that treating the lack of serotonin in the brain may temporarily improve symptoms of bulimia nervosa. However, there is no real evidence that people with eating disorders are carbohydrate addicts. Overall ratios of carbohydrate, fat and protein are pretty normal in most sufferers. Many people with body image disorders believe they are consuming vast quantities of carbohydrates, but actually the ratios are not abnormal, it is the emotions that are abnormal. The problem lies in the sense of loss of control, rather than food composition.

I would certainly not dismiss the addictions model entirely. Some aspects of addictions treatments seem to work for some people. In my opinion, the idea of body image disorders as addictions can be a helpful metaphor, but does not really explain the totality of the problem. Having said that, anything that helps you understand your condition and to recover is fine by me. The 12-steps approach to eating disorders, using an addictions model, has had very impressive results in many patients.

Chapter 12

The role of culture

'Fat is not just a feminist issue'

From the moment we began to publish studies on men and body image problems, I was invited to participate in a number of public debates on the subject. Most of these debates were constructed to generate maximum disagreement, which is a sensible strategy for journalistic attention and much more entertaining than agreement. In a commentary published in the *Lancet*, I had entitled the article 'Fat is not just a Feminist Issue'. This was misconstrued as representing a confrontation between men and women, even an attack on feminism. I could never bring myself to engage in the confrontation, or even accept that it exists. Most of my clinical practice is spent in treating women with eating disorders. Fat *is* a feminist issue. Women are more likely than men to suffer from eating disorders, and body image disparagement is usually more common amongst women. However, men are rapidly closing the gap and male body image insecurity is being stoked through the media and advertising. In stating that men are suffering, I am not stating that women are not suffering.

There are important biological, as well as cultural, differences between men and women. We carried out research on 'intersex' conditions, in which children are biologically female but with brains steeped in male hormones before birth. We looked at their development into adulthood and published our findings in the *British Medical Journal* in 2005. Interestingly, we found that they were happy, balanced, sane and socially adjusted individuals, but with a proclivity for non-feminine gender orientation. The 'male' hormones do make a difference to children with intersex conditions. Masculinity is not just a cultural construct, but hugely embedded in biology. Contemporary society has a problem with aspects of masculinity.

Ask any mother the 'nature vs. nurture' question, and she would regard the answer as obvious. Boys will be boys, and girls will be girls, with lots of marvellous hinterland between. Gender stereotyping cannot be entirely blamed for all these differences. Culture alters the way in which masculinity is expressed, but biology sets the agenda. How do these differences between boys and girls affect the development of eating disorders and body image disorders?

We know much more about gender, culture and women's eating problems. Studies show that the majority of perfectly normal women consistently regard themselves as overweight when in fact they are appropriately sized. From an early age, women experience a moral dimension to appetitive behaviour. Larger women are not just regarded as unattractive, but also as lacking moral fibre. The link between morality and appetitive behaviour is commonly applied to women in many different societies, and eating disorders are one manifestation of a worldwide phenomenon. Suppression of appetitive function in women is regarded not just as physically desirable, but virtuous. In the tenth century, Saint Wilgefortis rejected a politically motivated marriage to a man she did not love, and instead took herself to a convent where she starved to such an extent that she grew the bodily hair (Lanugo) found in some people with anorexia nervosa. This hair growth was seen as a miracle of God, and fasting cults spread throughout Europe in imitation. Turning to the twenty-first century, where once a woman with anorexia nervosa might be regarded as spiritually perfect, now she would rightly be regarded as in need of treatment. But lesser degrees of self-starvation are still seen as signs of physical and moral achievement.

Men have been relatively immune to these influences until recently. But images of men portrayed in the media are starting to resemble the worst excesses of female body image objectification. Men's magazines frequently show headlines that suggest moral virtue associated with a 'six-pack', high income, culinary expertise and sexual prowess. By implication, you don't make the grade if you can't balance an array of impossible aspirations.

Men's attitude to male weight and shape is a confused picture. Men who are underweight can be regarded with a certain fascination. Scrawny or skinny men may be portrayed as lacking power, potency and prowess. Men are increasingly exposed to impossible body image ideals, compatible only with excessive exercise or steroid misuse. AIDS and HIV added new complexity to male body image ideals, insofar as heightened muscular definition became an aspiration, particularly in the gay community. Whereas most women aspire to weight loss, men present a far more confused picture. Almost half of all men wish to lose significant amounts of weight, but the other half aspire to weight gain. Weight gain really signifies muscle bulk. Whereas women will set themselves weight loss targets, men will be less concerned with the weighing scales and more concerned with body shape. These gender differences generate confusion when it comes to diagnosing eating disorders in men, where many specialists are used to discussing the fear of normal body weight more than the desire to 'resculpt' the body.

Whilst the average middle-aged man is quite tolerant of his overweight, the situation appears very different among young men and boys. We carried out a study of male body image among young college students, and found frightening levels of body image disparagement. Many aspire to the sculptured and overdeveloped bodies so commonly espoused in men's magazines. To acquire a six-pack requires hours of training spread over years, beyond the reach of most people with well-balanced lives. The shortcut involves either an imbalanced life, or misuse of anabolic steroids (as discussed in Chapter 9). The fact that so many young men are now using illegal anabolic steroids is a serious concern, but a hidden epidemic. Of course, some aspects of the male body image ideal are desirable. This contrasts with the excessively thin female body image ideal, so at odds with a normal female physiology. The male ideal is the testosterone-driven mesomorphic (triangular) look which, in moderation, does signify one version of health. The desire for a six-pack is simply an extreme expression of avoidance of layers of abdominal fat, in itself a sign of health. We know that waist girth is a particular predictor of early heart attack, such that a slim waist is certainly a sign of health, and signs of health are generally attractive. Like peacocks growing such long tail feathers that they cannot run, these outward signs of vigour and prowess become so exaggerated that they actually indicate the opposite of what they seek to portray. The slim waist of the man with anorexia nervosa or the excessively developed body musculature of muscle dysmorphia are both caricatures of culturally endorsed perfection.

Ultimately, it is unnatural for societies to present a single body image ideal. Men and women come in all shapes and sizes, and those shapes and sizes will be attractive to someone, somewhere. Discrimination against men because of body shape is growing just as unrelentingly as discrimination against women. The tall muscular man is more likely to be seen as attractive, to gain a better job, to hold a more powerful position in society and earn a higher salary. Judging men on appearance alone is just as insidious as in women, but awareness of the latter has been rightly heightened by feminism. Men have not yet reached the same enlightened position. This isn't just a problem for men. Who wants to live in such a superficial society? Many of my feminist friends now have to address the very real and immediate insecurities of young men, as they become mothers of sons. We should accept no body image ideals beyond health, balance and respect for diversity.

Part IV

Seven stages to recovery

I will go on to describe a programme of treatment that is tried and tested. For some men, they may dip in and out of the different stages. You may find some parts more useful than others. For example, you may find that the third stage (healthy habits), aimed at identifying and changing your behaviours, suits you more than the fifth stage (feeling good), aimed at looking at your feelings and your relationships with other people. You may find that you begin to adopt the recommendations of the treatment, but lose motivation after a while, and only return to the programme when you have time and space to do so. You may start off full of good intentions but become frustrated or upset with what is being asked of you. This is usual and normal. Your ability to tolerate and work through these feelings makes all the difference. The seven stages are as follows:

- **Stage 1: Motivation**. A cost-benefit analysis of recovery. Here you are asked to look at your motives for proceeding with the programme and anticipate the promises and pitfalls that await.
- **Stage 2: Sharing the secret**. At this stage, we explore the possibility of talking to family and friends, and the use they may be to you on your road to recovery.
- **Stage 3: Healthy habits**. At this stage you are asked to examine your behaviours, either in relation to eating or to exercise, by means of a diary, and then to change those behaviours.
- **Stage 4: Thinking straight**. This stage draws on the theories of cognitive therapy and problem-solving therapy (RASCAL) to examine the thoughts that may be driving your behaviours.
- **Stage 5: Feeling good**. At this stage you are ready to examine your feelings and interpersonal relations. Here we discuss aspects of inter-personal therapy, a form of psychotherapy of proven value in eating disorders and related body image disorders.
- **Stage 6: Seeking help**. For many men with eating disorders, and indeed most with anorexia nervosa, professional help is a necessary aspect of recovery. In this chapter I attempt to guide you through the process

of seeking professional help as an active 'consumer' rather than a passive participant.

- **Stage 7: Remaining well**. Once recovered, there is always the risk of relapse further down the line. This chapter lays out some of the principles of relapse prevention.

If you are anything like me, you may skim through the chapters in any old order, picking up titbits along the way but not actually sitting down and studying it. If so, *the three most critical stages are Stages 3, 4 and 5*: identifying and changing your behaviours (Healthy habits), exploring the thoughts behind those behaviours (Thinking straight) and examining your emotions (Feeling good). This is the essence of the treatment programme and involves the most work. It is not enough to simply read these chapters, but instead you need to implement them. These will teach you everything you need to know to break the cycle of self-destruction.

Chapter 13

Stage 1: Motivation

A cost-benefit analysis of recovery

In this chapter, you are asked to consider your *true* motivation to change, using a practical cost-benefit approach. Eating disorders and also muscle dysmorphia are adaptive. They can help you cope with the world. They are not just problems, but also solutions to problems. Stage 1 asks you to examine and anticipate what you will lose as well as what you will gain by proceeding with the programme. We know that this makes it more likely you will persist with the full programme.

> When I first decided to tackle my eating disorder, I had already done a lot of reading around the subject. I knew all about the damage that I had done to my body, and it made me quite frightened. I think I probably knew more about eating disorders than my doctor!
>
> But when it actually came to practical steps, I just couldn't do it. I realised my eating problems did affect my relationship with my mum, that my career had been suffering and that all my mates were leaving me behind; getting married, having children, basically able to do all the things I couldn't.
>
> But when it actually boiled down to gaining weight, reducing my exercise and then looking at myself in the mirror, I just couldn't do it. I think other people had panicked, and rushed me into treatment, but my head wasn't ready for it. I should have done more thinking.

Psychiatrists and psychologists talk about insight. Insight sounds like a pretty straightforward idea. You know that hitting yourself over the head with a hammer is bad for you. Unfortunately, body image disorders aren't like that. Eating disorders and muscle dysmorphia are ego-syntonic, in harmony with your sense of self. In other words, they arise from you as a person. They are a part of you and not instantly recognisable as a problem, but rather as a solution to a problem.

Men with eating disorders are often high achievers, highly intelligent and very well read. They can have a deep intellectual understanding of the nature of their disorder, fully accepting the theory at an intellectual level, but struggling to apply it to themselves. Deciding to confront your body image problem or eating disorder therefore confronts this sense of self. There are losses as well as gains.

Seeing the wood for the trees

How to do a cost-benefit analysis

Imagine that you are struggling with the decision about buying a new car. On the one hand, you have your eye on a rather expensive Japanese model sports car that's just outside of your budget, but you feel you should be rewarded for all the hard work you've been doing in the last few years. On the other hand, you're already in a bit of debt, you'd like to be saving cash in the long term to put down as a deposit on a house, and in any case you can rarely drive more than 20 miles an hour on your daily commute.

If you were trying to make your mind up over such a trivial decision, you might make the following steps. First, you might sit down and draw up a cost-benefit analysis. You might list all the pluses and all the minuses between buying a car in the short term and buying a house in the long term. You might then look at the strength of each of those pros and cons. For example, there might be eight really good reasons not to buy the sports car, and one really good reason why you should. But the last reason might far outweigh the first eight, and so you would decide to go ahead.

Second, you might use your imagination. In an idle moment, you might simply sit down and fantasise about what it would be like to have the car. You might imagine driving on open roads in a summer morning. You might imagine a sense of pride at seeing it parked outside your front door. Then you might start to fantasise about owning your own home, what it would feel like not paying rent, walking through the door for the first time. Third, you might talk these things through with family or friends, getting a better sense of perspective.

These are all strategies that you could, and should, apply when you are thinking of making decisions about your eating disorder or body image problem. However, studies suggest that we are much better able to take a rational, dispassionate approach to relatively trivial issues than the big ones. Big issues have so much emotion invested in them that we stop 'seeing the wood for the trees'.

The science

There is a whole discipline of health psychology that studies how people make decisions to change behaviours. The work of two experts in the field, Miller and Rollnick, helped to develop a form of therapy called 'motivational enhancement', and this has had a dramatic impact, based on hard factual evidence. There are many studies on why people decide to change, how they deal with ambivalence, and also what stages they pass through in order to make decisions. Bringing ambivalence out into the open is particularly helpful in managing body image disorders. Strategies for addressing ambivalence and motivation are critical. Specialist services that spend time and energy on addressing motivational enhancement are far better than services that simply plunge patients into treatment, without thinking things through in advance.

There is increasing evidence for the benefits of motivational enhancement therapy in the field of eating disorders. Among many others, Josie Geller in Canada and Janet Treasure and Ulrike Schmidt in the UK have been at the forefront of applying these techniques to eating disorders. More recently we have been studying involvement of families in motivational enhancement therapy. Men with eating disorders or other body image problems may fall within four basic categories, according to their level of motivation and insight. There are technical terms for these states of mind, but they can be summed up as:

- No way
- OK maybe
- Go for it
- Keep it up.

It is worth taking some time to understand these categories, and how they might apply to you. However, a word of warning: none of us is very good about making such judgements about ourselves.

No way: Pre-contemplation

People who are pre-contemplative do not even necessarily regard themselves as having a problem. Your mother complains that you are losing weight, and people at work start to make critical comments. You've spent all your money on expensive gym subscriptions, or your friends are beginning to leave you alone because they don't understand your weight loss. But you yourself don't think there is anything wrong at all. At the pre-contemplative stage, it would be normal to perceive the problem as lying with your mum or with your friends, not with yourself. You aren't really keen to do anything about these matters, because you don't think you have a problem at all. Other people have the problem.

OK maybe: Contemplation

If you are reading *The Invisible Man* at all, it is likely that you have reached this stage. At the contemplative stage you are beginning to consider that there may be a problem. You may have not yet decided that it is a problem you can, or want, to tackle but you do recognise that something is going on. In the contemplative stage, ambivalence is maximum. You are beginning to think 'on the one hand, on the other hand'. For example, you may be thinking:

> Well, if I gained some weight my physical health would be so much better. I would be able to concentrate more at work. I am sick of being so preoccupied with eating and exercise rituals. I'd like to start to tackle the issues. However, if I do begin to tackle these issues I will have to think about reducing my exercise. I just couldn't imagine not going to the gym after work. I don't want my stomach to go all flabby or my face to balloon.

Most people in my clinic are presenting at this stage of recovery, though quite a number are still at a pre-contemplative stage.

If you are reading *The Invisible Man* as someone's relative, it may well be that your loved one is still in the pre-contemplative stage. In that instance, you can act as an important instigator for change. This doesn't mean bullying, chivvying and criticising. Rather, the best way to move someone from pre-contemplative to contemplative is by being as neutral as possible, or what has been termed 'collaborative empiricism'.

Go for it: Action

Imagine you have now decided to buy your shiny red sports car. You've been fantasising and dreaming about it for ages, but now you're ready to make a move. You decide to visit the car showroom that weekend, and you have the money ready in your account, albeit you borrowed a lot of it from your uncle. You're now ready to make a move.

Suddenly the decision becomes more real. It might change the judgements from your cost-benefit analysis. You begin to consider the reality of being in debt. New problems emerge in your head. You live in a pretty rough area and, if you park the car outside your house, you know that one day someone will scratch it. You have just read a report indicating that the particular model was one of the most unreliable on the market, and you won't have cash to get repairs done. Also spare parts are extremely expensive.

As you move from contemplation to action, things get a lot more personal. Things get a lot more real. The losses and gains of your decision become accentuated in your mind. You make a commitment to change your behaviours and thoughts and you 'go for it'. This is where the real works begins. For example, if your eating disorder is a means of dealing with other more subtle problems, those problems may become accentuated.

You may have a sense of low self-esteem that predates the onset of your body image disorder. Being able to control your diet and body has been your way of feeling good about yourself, however tenuous and unsustainable the approach. Suddenly you have to confront not just the changes in your body, but also the reasons for your low self-esteem in the first place. Some people get bogged down in the quagmire of their thoughts. Sometimes thinking too much can be the biggest obstacle to the action stage:

> Once upon a time there was a millipede. He lived a simple life in a beautiful forest, and every day he would walk along the road from his home under a big log to the little clearing in the forest where he worked.
>
> One day he walked past a lazy beetle, who had always been a bit of a bully. The beetle looked him up and down disparagingly and said: 'How on earth do you manage to walk with all your legs? How do you coordinate them? When do you decide to move the ones on the right and the ones on the left? Who needs so many legs? That's just silly!'
>
> The millipede tried to ignore him, but couldn't help thinking about what he had said. He began to think about all his legs and how he made them move. The more he thought, the harder it was to coordinate himself. He started to trip over himself. Should he move the ones on the right first and the ones on the left next, or should he be moving the ones at the front first and the ones at the back next? The more he thought, the less he was able to continue walking, until eventually he just fell over in a tangle of legs and never got up again.

This can happen in the action phase of therapeutic change. You try to start to do something, but your thinking gets in the way and you end up like the millipede, on your back with your legs kicking up in the air.

That is why the *OK maybe* stage of change is very important. If you move into the *Go for it* stage too quickly, without thinking through the pros and cons, you can end up trapped in this state of useless thought and prevarication. For this reason, men don't meekly pass through each of the four stages of change, and it is not uncommon to move backwards and forwards:

> James first presented with anorexia nervosa when he was 16 years old. He was forced to see his GP by his mother, and denied any eating disorder behaviours whatsoever. He knew he was concealing the truth from his mum and his doctor, but there was no way he could tell them what was really going on. The doctor was concerned that he might be suffering from some sort of physical problem, and he was investigated for a range of possible illnesses. They did blood tests and tests for infections and they all came back negative.

All of this took two years and, by the end, James had started to look forward to leaving home and going to university. He found that this was sufficient to get himself to gain a bit of weight. Without having got to the bottom of his problem, both his doctor and his mother decided that whatever it was had gone away, and that appeared to be the end of the matter.

However, three years later one of his friends was killed in a car accident. James was far more upset than he had expected. He started thinking about his own life and whether he really wanted to carry on in the career that he had chosen.

His old ways of anorexia nervosa came back and this time things really spiralled out of control, until he was at an extremely low weight. He was admitted to a medical ward where again he denied his problems. However, a psychiatrist visited him on the ward and asked him the SCOFF questions as well as some pretty straightforward direct questions about calorie consumption, exercise and slimming pills.

Eventually it all came out, and for the first time he received a clear-cut diagnosis of anorexia nervosa. Whilst he accepted it at an intellectual level, at an emotional level he didn't quite see the diagnosis as belonging to him. It felt unreal. He thought of anorexia nervosa as a condition that woman suffered. Nonetheless he recognised something was wrong, and he accepted that 'something should be done about it'.

Rather reluctantly he agreed to attend an outpatient clinic where he saw a clinical psychologist. The psychologist was very probing and very understanding, and over a period of six months he gradually felt himself able to open up and trust enough to talk not just about his problems with eating, but also experiences of being bullied at school, and the difficult relationship he had had with his father.

With the psychologist's expertise, he recognised the need to gain some weight, and was put on a nutritional rehabilitation programme in which he attempted to gain half a kilogram a week. This went very well for the first three months, but as he approached a BMI of around 18 he began to feel very differently about himself and his body. His feelings became much more complicated than they had been at the beginning. He couldn't quite say whether he was feeling sad, angry, depressed or panicky. His feelings didn't make much sense to him at all, but it was a horrible position to be in, and almost without thinking about it he began to lose weight again. He also began to clam up in therapy and missed appointments.

Unfortunately at this stage his clinical psychologist went on an extended period of maternity leave, and the person standing in for her was really not at all his 'cup of tea'. He stopped attending the clinic altogether, and although he received a number of letters from the clinic he just didn't bother to respond. Eventually he moved out of the area and got a clerical job.

For the next few years he kept his head down, and somehow managed to maintain a stable but low weight. He convinced himself he was happy, although on the few occasions when he really looked deeply into himself he would acknowledge that he had a far more limited life than he had hoped for. One day he went on holiday with some friends. It was a last-minute decision, but it had a lasting effect on his life. He met a woman in Greece called Lisa, and they fell in love. They carried on seeing each other when they came home. Initially he would avoid staying over with Lisa because it might be difficult to explain some of the behaviours and rituals he had around food. However, it was already obvious to Lisa that something was up.

She asked him all about it, and he told her how every day of his life he was taking slimming pills, how he would avoid taking off his clothes in front of her but rather get undressed under the duvet, how he would always leave the house early in the morning in order to go to the gym, and how often when they went out to dinner together he would sneak off and make himself sick.

Because he was disgusted with himself, he expected Lisa to share that disgust. Instead she listened calmly and patiently without pushing too much. They carried on talking about the problems and eventually Lisa persuaded him to seek help. Because it was so hard to get expert help, Lisa got in touch with the Beat, the eating disorder association, and found a list of specialist units. James agreed to treatment at a specialist unit, but struggled to gain weight in the outpatient department. He was eventually admitted as an inpatient. He did extremely well, and Lisa developed such a good understanding of his problems that she continued to motivate him even after his discharge.

Although this case is fictional, it does represent a very typical scenario. The journey from *No way* to *OK maybe* and then *Go for it* can take months or years. I have seen people presenting in complete denial of their problem, but then big life events like a new relationship completely alter their perspective and motivation to change. In the story of James, you can see someone reposition themselves from *No way* to *OK maybe* and *Go for it*, but also moving backwards again. Self-awareness is the key to recovery in eating disorders. Ask yourself which stage you are at now.

Keep it up: Maintenance

Maintenance is the final stage in recovery, and in many ways the most difficult stage. After a flurry of interest from health-care professionals, suddenly you are on your own trying to avoid relapse. Good specialist services for body image and eating disorders will focus energy on this stage. It is all very well helping someone recover, but maintaining recovery is the tricky bit. Keeping in the maintenance phase involves a focus on trigger factors that might cause you to deteriorate. In identifying those factors, you can learn from the past. What made things worse in the past is likely to make things worse in the future. I address this in more detail in Chapter 9 – Stage 7 of treatment (sadder and wiser).

Practical exercises

Set aside at least an hour of undisturbed time when you can sit alone in a room. Bring several clean sheets of paper and a pen. First, think about your own progress. Do you think you are really ready to 'Go for it'? Are you more realistically thinking 'OK maybe'? Don't accept the first thought that goes through your head. Put it to the test. For example, can you imagine enduring a day without going to the gym? What would it feel like? Could you cope, or would you convince yourself otherwise? Consider this not just in terms of intellectual insight, but also your emotional responses.

Second, start to visualise your thoughts and intentions as a battleground between two very different camps. On one side is the 'healthy' camp, filled with an armoury of good intentions, self-knowledge and will power, driven by a host of reasons for getting better. Think about that camp and try to list its strengths. On the other side is the 'ill' camp, also filled with strengths. Visualise all the things that keep you ill.

Without necessarily trying to argue against your 'ill' self, try to identify all the thoughts you've had in the last ten minutes while reading *The Invisible Man*. Some of those thoughts belong to your 'healthy' camp and others belong to your 'ill' camp. Don't censor yourself and don't try too hard to argue whether the thoughts are right or wrong. Once you do that, you will find yourself minimising and distorting things. Be completely neutral and non-judgemental. Just write them down and try to classify them into the two different camps.

Look at your list. It doesn't have to be extensive. Work out which are the really big issues and which are the small ones. For example, in your ill camp, 'There's no way I would go a week without going to the gym' may seem like a huge issue, whereas 'I don't particularly like being told what to do' may seem smaller. In your healthy camp, 'I really want to have a decent relationship for a change' may seem the huge issue, whereas 'I spend too much money on slimming pills' may feel less important.

Next, try to think about your feelings for those two camps. Take a piece of paper, and write a list separately addressing both of them. For one heading, write 'This is what I like about you'. For another heading write 'This is what I hate about you'. You might end up with something looking like this:

I love the way I feel after I've been working out. I look in the mirror and have a sense of real achievement. I like the feeling in the evening when I've eaten virtually nothing all day. I go to bed feeling so fuzzy in my head, thinking 'Yes, I've been able to do it again.'

I hate the way I can never go out for meals with other people. I hate my anorexia because it's made me lose all my friends. I feel so weird about my body, about never being able to look into a mirror.

Don't be embarrassed or inhibited by this. Remember, you can tear up all this paper afterwards and no one will ever see it. By now you will be starting to have a sense of what you gain by remaining ill, and what you might lose by getting better. Hopefully, you will also be having a sense of what you are losing by remaining ill, and what you will gain by getting better.

Begin to turn this into a proper list. Focus on the benefits of recovery from your eating disorder or body image problem. You might think of this in terms of the following domains: *physical, emotional, relationships*, and *quality of life*. For example, if you suffer from anorexia nervosa and apply this, you may think along the following lines:

1   Weight gain would help my mobility and concentration. I would be physically strong enough to go on more trips out.
2   I might become more like the person I used to be, with more self-confidence and ambition.
3   I might have fewer arguments with my mum about things, and she would no longer be worrying so much.
4   I could contemplate resigning from my current job, and moving to a new job in central England where my sister lives. If I was able to move, a lot of the stress would be taken away from my life and I could really put my life back on track again.

If you suffer from bulimia nervosa you might be thinking along the following lines:

1   Once I stop myself being sick, I will gradually find my body going back to normal. My teeth would get better, and I wouldn't be embarrassed about seeing the dentist. Maybe I wouldn't feel drained of energy all the time if I wasn't taking laxatives.
2   If I could stop bingeing, I'd feel less impulsive. I'm sick of riding an emotional rollercoaster and being ratty with everyone. I could be open and honest about things, instead of hiding things away.

3   I could have a more normal social life, maybe go for meals with my mates and spend more time thinking about things that matter to me rather than boring things like the calorie content of food or how I will manage to make myself puke after every meal.
4   I could do more with my friends, go on holiday with them to Cornwall, and maybe take my younger brother to the match.
5   All the money I save from buying food I don't even want, I could save it up and buy myself an old car.

If you suffer from muscle dysmorphia, you might be thinking along the following lines.

1   If I let my body rest a bit more, I wouldn't be always suffering from pulled muscles. I could really let my Achilles recover. Maybe I wouldn't get so many coughs and colds.
2   If I stop taking steroids, maybe I wouldn't lose my temper all the time. I would feel more in control over my emotions.
3   Maybe I could tell my brother what has really been happening to me, whereas at the moment we're not even talking to each other. He's still a young lad, and doesn't understand why I've been so irritable and angry. Even if I don't tell him, I'd like to patch things up before it's too late.
4   Instead of spending three hours in the gym every day, I would get involved in the World Wildlife Fund again, rejoin the committee and do something useful for other people rather than just myself.

What you might lose by getting better

It is just as important to prepare yourself for negatives as well as positives. Recovery does involve losses as well as gains. You should acknowledge and anticipate these disadvantages just as openly as the advantages. They belong in the camp of your enemy, and give it strength. You need to know your enemy in order to fight him. Bring the losses out into the open. Write them down on a separate piece of paper. Think about them fully and honestly.

Then put that piece of paper down and go back to the gains. Imagine a life without your body image disorder. Imagine you have a healthy, normal relationship with food and exercise. Don't just think that in the abstract. Shut your eyes and try to 'be' that person. Go back to the list of 'losses' and see if they are now eclipsed by the real-life experience of the gains. If you can do this, and repeat the exercise, you can move yourself from being a 'No way' or 'Maybe if' kind of guy, and become a 'Go for it'.

'If you can meet with triumph and disaster, and treat those two impostors just the same'

This isn't just a paper exercise. Dealing with issues of motivation is essential for recovery. Many men I have treated have started out with a sense of powerlessness about their thoughts and feelings, as if they were beyond their control. But there is good evidence that you can change the way you see yourself and others by this means. This doesn't just apply in body image disorders. There has been considerable research looking at the motivations behind highly successful athletes and high-achieving leaders. The 'go for it' attitude, ability to see 'the wood for the trees' and avoidance of prevarication seem to be at the route of success. Not only that, but you can learn to think in the same way.

For some people, reading a self-help book like this may be sufficient in itself. For some, sharing the secret with family and friends can be extremely beneficial. However, some men with body image disorders are so overwhelmed by motivational issues that seeking professional help becomes essential. Chapter 18 on Stage 6 of the recovery guide ('Seeking Professional Help – A Consumer's Guide') covers this particular phase in greater detail.

Finally, what really distinguishes people who recover from those who do not? It isn't the ability to comply with all the suggestions in *The Invisible Man* and so pass smoothly through each stage of recovery. It is much more about how you deal with triumph and disaster. You can afford to have a 'bad day' if you have the mental strength to maintain your motivation, dust yourself down and get on with it. Maintaining your motivation despite failure is more important than success.

Chapter 14

Stage 2: Sharing the secret

For many of my patients, confiding in family or friends is critical in recovery. Telling friends that you have an eating disorder may not surprise them. Often these matters have been an open secret for months or years. Making the issues explicit can come as a tremendous relief to everyone. Families and close friends can be powerful allies in the fight against these dreadful illnesses. As I write this book, several leading experts in the field of eating disorders are experimenting with the training of family and friends to act as 'therapists'. However, this only works if you stand shoulder to shoulder. Therefore it is important to consider timing and context of sharing the secret.

Tolerating and listening

There are pros and cons. Think them through before you act. Most often, your family can be a solution to your problem, but in some cases family relations may be strained as a result of your illness. Family and friends may have strong feelings of anger, sadness, confusion and helplessness. If you consider how hard it has been for you to help yourself, consider how hard it could be for your loved ones to watch you battle with a life-threatening illness over which they have no control. The most common question I receive from the relatives and friends of men with body image disorders is 'What do I do?' It is usually not a question of doing, but rather of tolerating and listening.

If you decide to share your secret, do remember that friends and relatives are as fallible as you. There are no right answers, and it is inevitable that they will say or do things that irritate or inflame you.

Make a wish list

Try and think of practical suggestions. Make a wish list of ten things. Everything on that list should be a clear action point, not an open-ended plea. For example, you might know that Sundays are your riskiest time for behaviours to assert themselves. You might therefore suggest: 'It would be good if sometimes I could go to the cinema on Sunday evenings with you, and then have a meal together.' This is far more helpful than something non-specific, such as 'I want you to listen to me'.

After you have constructed your wish list, go back over it. Remember that two quite distinct forces dominate your thinking. Your 'healthy' self will be encouraging you to overcome your illness. Your 'pathological' self will be pushing in the opposite direction. For example, if you suffer from anorexia nervosa, you might find that some of your wish list is looking for family and friends to collude with your illness. 'I want you to let me eat my dinners on my own' may appear as a cry for independence, but you might actually be looking for the chance to restrict your diet or make yourself vomit in privacy. Therefore try to re-examine your wish list with a critical eye and consider whether any of those suggestions represent your 'ill' self.

Jim's story

Jim is a 22-year-old man with a five-year history of anorexia nervosa. Having graduated with a good English degree from university, he found he was simply not coping away from home, and so he has been living with his mum and stepdad for the past year.

He has hinted to his mother that he is having problems with eating but she misinterpreted what he was saying and assumed he meant that he had lost his appetite. As a result, she suggested they should all go on family walks on Sundays.

He has never got on very well with his stepfather who he feels is 'always hassling me about getting a job'. At times the arguments really flare up and he finds his stepfather physically threatening. However, more often than not the problems simply simmer beneath the surface. No one in the family says what they are really thinking. Everything is hinted and implied.

Jim's sister, Suzanne, has described the atmosphere as 'poisonous' and has happily gone on a 'gap year' to Australia. Jim used to feel very close to his mother, particularly when he was a teenager, but somehow he finds it very difficult to speak to her. Jim would like to tell his mother about his eating disorder.

Jim goes to the library, with a great big pad and pen, where he knows he won't be disturbed. He writes down on a piece of paper the pros and cons of telling his mother about his eating disorder.

PROS

1   I think that she already knows that I have an eating disorder, and it will probably help her understand some of my behaviours.

2   The arguments during family meals make it even harder for me to eat regularly. Perhaps if mum understood things better it would be possible to eat in a relaxed and more controlled way.

3   I already feel stupid and useless because I don't have a job, and at least my stepdad might begin to understand why I am not working. It's not because I am lazy.

4   I don't think I am ready to try to gain weight, but I am particularly concerned about taking laxatives, I feel a physical wreck and I am worried that I may be harming my body. I am frightened of going to the GP on my own, and it would be useful if mum could come with me.

5   I don't think mum has ever understood how upset I have felt since the divorce. I miss my real dad and I wish I could see more of him.

CONS

1   I don't think my stepdad is capable of changing himself or his character. He will just think that I am weak willed or something, or maybe even try to force me into hospital.

2   Mum has enough on her plate with her own worries, without needing to be bogged down with mine.

3   It's a lot easier to ignore what's happening, whereas if I bring it out into the open people will start to want me to change and I don't think I am able to do that.

4   I feel like I have lost my sister already and, if she realises how weird I am, she will become even more distant.

Jim then examines his various statements, and tries to dissect them. For example, he begins to understand how many of the cons he has listed are actually his illness speaking. He recognises that ignoring a problem doesn't mean that the problem doesn't exist. However, he also recognises that this is the strategy he has always adopted, and is typical of his family in general.

On the other hand, he is able to recognise that he really isn't ready to attempt a full recovery from his eating disorder. He has rather more limited aims to reduce his laxative intake and stabilise his eating pattern, without necessarily attempting weight gain. He thinks he can only achieve this by seeing his GP, but needs his mother's help.

Thus, when he starts to weigh up the pros and cons, he decides that it is probably better to tell his mother than to go it alone, despite the problems that might arise. Next, he thinks about what he might say to his mum and how he might say it. He knows that she really has no understanding at all of eating disorders, and particularly of eating disorders in men. He tries to make a list of practical suggestions he might make to his mum in order to improve matters. Here are five of them:

1   I know you have your own life to lead and I don't want to become dependent on you, but it would be nice if we could have a bit more time together, just the two of us. When I was little we used to like going to the botanical gardens together. Perhaps we could try to do that once a month, and then eat a Sunday meal together in the café.
2   Could you come along with me to an appointment with my GP, and help me think of what I am going to ask him?
3   I cannot bring myself to eat dinner as a family just now, but I would like to try to eat breakfast regularly. It would help me if we could eat breakfast together in the morning, and plan what we are going to eat the day before.
4   My stepdad and I just can't get on, and we never will.
5   Some of the things you've suggested, like taking more exercise on Sunday, are actually going to make the problem worse, since over-exercising is one of my problems.

Jim then looks back over those questions and tries to tease apart the helpful from the harmful, or non-specific, ones. He thinks most of his suggestions are fairly practical, easy for mother to deliver and would make a real impact on his quality of life. On the other hand some of the suggestions aren't really suggestions at all. They are statements of how he is feeling. Telling his mother that he doesn't like his stepdad won't really achieve anything. It will put his mum in an impossible position. Telling mum that she doesn't understand about eating disorders is a negative way of putting things.

Deciding to tell friends

Many men with chronic body image disorders will have become socially isolated as a result of their disorder. Confiding in friends can be particularly hard for men. Even men without eating disorders find it difficult to admit to problems. However, it may simply be a case of you creating your own values. Most of us have one or two people who have that aura of wisdom and strength which is so important in discussing sensitive matters. These may not necessarily be the people you regard as your very closest friends. Thus you need to choose confidants wisely. It can be easier to confide in friends than family and parents. Parents can be so involved in the issues that it is very hard to keep a sense of perspective, whereas a good friend may act as a neutral sounding board.

A friend's perspective

David's friend, Simon, has struggled against anorexia nervosa, and later bulimia, for the past five years. David describes what it was like from his perspective:

Being told

I have known Simon since we were at school together, although we were not particularly close friends. I got to know him better when we ended up at the same college, and I always thought he was a very successful and confident man. He seemed to be good at everything, but particularly at cross-country running.

However, I first saw the other side to him when we got very drunk together. I was quite shocked when he started to tell me that he felt life wasn't worth living. He wasn't actually suicidal, but he was clearly desperate. I think the turning point was the next day, when we were both really hung over. He acted very embarrassed and I think he expected me to run a mile. I have always taken people as they come, and so just blurted out to him that I was a bit worried about him. After that it all came tumbling out, how he had been treated for anorexia nervosa while we were at school together, how he was now making himself puke every day and taking slimming pills.

He told me how he had tried to run a cross-country race after starving himself for 24 hours and had collapsed. I had no idea what an eating disorder was, except what you read in the papers, and all I could think to tell him was to go and see his doctor, but I don't think that was the answer he was seeking.

I don't think he was seeking any answer; really, he just wanted to offload. It was actually really complimentary that he had told me. It showed that he trusted me and in many ways we became closer as a result. I even felt able to tell him some of the problems I had been having with my mum. We were chatting on a different level to the way you normally would with a friend down the pub.

What I did

I didn't do anything at all. I just carried on listening to him. After that first time, we would just meet up and it would be the normal beers and a video with some mates. But every so often he would tell me some more about what was going on. I remember once he told me he had cut himself with a razor blade, and I was really shocked. I must admit I got very angry with him, which probably wasn't the best thing to do, but it made him sit up and listen, and I don't think he ever did it again, or perhaps he was scared to tell me about it again.

Even when we moved to different parts of the country, we somehow stayed in touch, either by telephone or occasionally meeting up to go walking together. The strange thing is, I think it made our friendship a lot deeper than it had been. I mean, all my other friends, we tend to compete with each other and pretend we are better than each other. With Simon I was able to be more myself. I know I never have to put up a front, and actually he is a bloody good listener himself. I think the problems he has been tackling mean that he is better able to help others.

I know he is still struggling with his eating problems. He has gained some weight, which he says makes him look like a blob, but I think he has never looked healthier. I tried to do some reading about eating disorders, and started to make some suggestions to him about things he could do or not do. I don't think any of that was particularly helpful. I don't think he particularly wanted to be told what to do. He already knew what he should be doing. He really just needs someone to shoot ideas off, discuss things without judging him. If I ever had a problem, I know I could turn to him, and I hope he feels the same about me.

What to do if telling someone goes wrong?

It is virtually impossible to know how people will react when you tell them about your eating disorder. In my clinical experience, more people receive a positive, supportive reaction than they are expecting. You start to imagine a worst case scenario in your mind, and that becomes an obstacle for change. As with any important news, the first reaction you get may not mean much. This just reflects the sort of people they are, and how they deal with things. Some people might ask lots and lots of questions. Some people sit there and don't say anything. Some people may show intense emotion. This is just their way of dealing with a revelation. What really counts is the reaction after the information has sunk in.

After you have shared the secret, it may be best to let it settle in, and return to it a couple of days later. This gives your confidant the chance to assimilate things in their own minds. Occasionally you do get a reaction that is unhelpful or hostile. Mums and dads can find it hard to get things right. There is no rulebook for being a parent. Typical unhelpful reactions include: 'But men don't get eating disorders. I thought it was only women. This is self-inflicted. You are just weak', or the classic 'Just snap out of it'.

If you have never had an eating disorder, or never known anyone who has had an eating disorder, it can be very difficult to understand what is at stake. This is not helped by some commentaries in the media, which simply reinforce the notion that eating disorders are the preserve of models and actresses. Even people trained in medicine can have a poor grip on the problem. How much harder would it be if you know nothing about the illness at all? Whatever reaction you get, you have to pat yourself on the back for trying. Above all else, we are all responsible for our own actions. If your confidant is unable to cope with the information, that is their problem not yours. Remember that admitting your body image disorder to someone else is part of the process of admitting it to yourself. Hiding yourself away as an 'invisible man' can be your way of ignoring the problem altogether. Telling someone, no matter what their reaction, makes your problem visible, not just to others but also to yourself.

Chapter 15

Stage 3: Healthy habits

In this chapter, we explore how you can identify and change vicious cycles of behaviour, by means of a diary. We look at two types of diary, suitable for people with either eating disorders or with muscle dysmorphia and compulsive exercise. This stage looks at how you can then attempt to change those behaviours through practical commonsense steps such as meal planning. We look at the importance of being 'in the moment', of self-awareness and self-efficacy.

The cornerstone of establishing healthy habits in a body image disorder is the use of a behaviour diary. You are unlikely to get better if you are unable to comply with this one aspect of your treatment. In order to establish new habits, you must first become aware of your old ones. Most men who keep a behaviour diary experience this as deeply intrusive, precisely because it is bringing bad habits into your awareness. The more you resent it, the more it is needed! There can be a tendency to complete the diary in retrospect, allowing you to gloss over past events, or con yourself into thinking things are better than they are. However, the 'rules' of the diary are:

- You should carry it with you wherever you go.
- You should complete it when you carry out a particular behaviour.
- You should be brutally honest with yourself.
- You should avoid filling it out 'after the event'.

The whats and the whys

The diary is aimed to highlight what you are doing, and also why you are doing it. In that regard, emotions and thoughts are an important part of the recording process. You should be writing down the time and place of a particular behaviour, as well as a brief description, coupled to some documentation of how you felt about things, and what you were thinking at the time. You should also try to record the consequences of the behaviour.

Typically, a diary is completed over a seven-day period, and every seven days you should consider your aims and objectives for that week. At the end of seven days, you should then look back over the preceding week and judge which aims and objectives you have achieved and which you haven't. You can learn as much from your failures as your successes. You should also record any other achievements.

Slowly does it

There are two components to the diary:

- First, you become aware.
- Second, you then make changes.

A common mistake is to rush into change at the beginning, only to feel overwhelmed. I have seen many diaries end up in the rubbish bin because people try to run before they can walk.

By means of the diary, you will become more aware of the pattern of your behaviour. By means of this awareness, you will then be in a position to change that behaviour.

Scratch beneath the surface

Many men with weight difficulties in particular may have used a diary approach in the past and found it unhelpful. In fact, we know that simple food monitoring is rarely helpful and can inflame the situation. However, the process we are discussing involves scratching beneath the surface, and trying to form links between actions, thoughts and feelings. In a sense, your behaviour diary becomes a pocket therapist with whom you can communicate 24/7. You record what you are doing, why you are doing it and how you are feeling.

Examples of behaviour diaries

These behaviour diaries are yours to use as you deem fit. I have provided possible examples for use in people with bulimia nervosa or binge eating, anorexia nervosa, and muscle dysmorphia. You may photocopy these or change them according to your own wishes. Often the best ones are the diaries you have created for yourself.

Ideally, you should create a diary with seven sheets representing the seven days of the week. You should have it in a format that is easily carried and can be slipped into your pocket. In this way you will be able to take it everywhere: on the bus, in the cinema, down the gym. You should fill it out as you go. At the end of the three blank examples, I have provided an example of a completed behavioural diary as it might apply in someone with bulimia nervosa.

EATING DISORDER DIARY

You should take this diary with you *at all times*.

Instructions

> The diary is most usefully completed at the times **when you least wish to do so** (immediately following a binge).
>
> Each page represents a new day. This diary covers a week.
>
> You should document exactly what you eat or drink at the time when you consume it.
>
> You should tick the columns when you consider you have used forms of abnormal eating behaviour (for example, starving, bingeing or vomiting).
>
> You should record thoughts, feelings and consequences **at that moment in time**. These should be the feelings as you experience them, rather than after reflection.

This will be upsetting and annoying.

At the beginning of every week, list three aims for that week:

1. . . . .
2. . . . .
3. . . . .

At the beginning of every week, apply the RASCAL approach to solving relevant problems.

Review (list three current problems that you wish to tackle over the week):

1. . . . .
2. . . . .
3. . . . .

Analyse (consider their priority)

Solve (on a scrap of paper, think through all possible solutions to those problems)

Cost-benefit (now consider the pros and cons of each approach)

Act (describe your action)

Learn (describe the outcome)

Day . . . . Date . . . . / . . . . . . / 20 . .

S = Starvation (extreme calorific restriction)
B = Bingeing
V = Vomiting
L = Laxative misuse
E = Exercise

Time	Description of food	How much	Place	S	B	V	L	E	Thoughts	Feelings

At the end of every week, review your aims and list your achievements:

1 . . . .
2 . . . .
3 . . . .

Now consider your mental attitudes during this week. This should reflect the whole week, and not just the time you filled out the diary. This week, I have felt:

1 My weight has been on my mind:
   Not at all |————————————————| *All the time*
2 My body shape has been on my mind:
   Not at all |————————————————| *All the time*
3 The urge to restrict has been:
   Out of control |————————————————| *In control*
4 The urge to binge has been:
   Out of control |————————————————| *In control*
5 Food and meals have been on my mind:
   All the time |————————————————| *Not at all*
6 My life has been in control:
   Not at all |————————————————| *All the time*
7 My confidence in myself has been:
   Best it could be |————————————————| *Worst it could be*
8 My relationship with people has been:
   Worst it could be |————————————————| *Best it could be*
9 My weight has:
   Increased / Stayed the same / Decreased
10 I have eaten the right amount of food at the right mealtimes:
   Not at all |————————————————|

EXERCISE DIARY

You should take this diary with you *at all times*.

Instructions

The diary is most usefully completed at the times **when you least wish to do so** (immediately following a workout).

Each page represents a new day. This diary covers a week.

You should document exactly what exercise you carry out, and any associated behaviours such as over-eating, steroid misuse or misuse of other pills.

You should record thoughts, feelings and consequences **at that moment in time**. These should be the feelings as you experience them, rather than after reflection.

This will be upsetting and annoying.

At the beginning of every week, list three aims for that week:

1 . . . .
2 . . . .
3 . . . .

Day . . . . Date . . . . / . . . . . . / 20 . .

Time	Description of exercise	How much	Place	Associated behaviours*		Thoughts	Feelings

At the end of every week, review your aims and list your achievements:

1 . . . .
2 . . . .
3 . . . .

* Record here any abnormal eating behaviours such as bingeing / vomiting, use of steroids, and use of other pills.

Now consider your mental attitudes during this week. This should reflect the whole week, and not just the time you filled out the diary. This week, I have felt:

1 My body shape has been on my mind:
   Not at all |————————————————| *All the time*
2 My weight has been on my mind:
   Not at all |————————————————| *All the time*
3 The urge to exercise has been:
   Out of control |————————————————| *In control*
4 Food and meals have been on my mind:
   All the time |————————————————| *Not at all*
5 My life has been in control:
   Not at all |————————————————| *All the time*
6 My confidence in myself has been:
   Best it could be |————————————————| *Worst it could be*
7 My relationship with people has been:
   Worst it could be |————————————————| *Best it could be*
8 My weight has:
   Increased / Stayed the same / Decreased

Tips on completing the diaries

Time

You should accurately record the time of particular behaviours, including abnormal and normal eating behaviour. For many people there is a pattern in their behaviour, and links can be made between certain times and certain events. For example, some men find their eating behaviours are relatively normal during the working day, but in the evening the pattern becomes more pathological. Many men with bulimia nervosa will consume an inadequate breakfast, such that binge eating is provoked by extreme starvation later in the day. The absence of regular normal meals is often associated with the presence of more bulimic eating. In muscle dysmorphia, the compulsion to exercise may be confined to evenings.

Description of food or exercise

You should write down as simply and quickly as possible just exactly what you have eaten or what exercise you have performed. Do not record the quantity at this stage, but rather a very brief characterisation of its substance. It is very easy to 'rewrite history' by filling this out retrospectively.

This must be avoided if the behavioural diary is to be successful. Where your problem is muscle dysmorphia, instead you will be completing a description of the exercise behaviour, but using the same format.

Quantity

Here you should give a very brief description of quantities. Do not write too much. Sometimes such diaries can actually tap into underlying obsessional ruminations and it is particularly in recording quantities that this can be most apparent.

Location

Many behavioural patterns become fixed around certain locations. For example, you may find it relatively easy to eat in the office canteen, but much more difficult to eat in your own bedroom. Eating in the bedroom may be particularly associated with abnormal eating behaviours. Your home may be a 'safe place' in terms of compulsive exercise. A simple record of location allows this pattern to become apparent.

B = binge eating

Here you should record with a simple tick or cross whether the food consumed represented a binge. We have discussed the formal and technical definition of a binge elsewhere. Here you are recording your personal sense of the behaviour, and particularly the sense of being out of control.

V = vomiting

Here you record any purging behaviour, including self-induced vomiting. If there are particular behaviours that are part of your own abnormal repertoire, then you can also record them here, annotating the diary accordingly. Fit the diary around you, not vice versa.

L = laxatives

Record laxative misuse in a separate column. We often find that purging behaviours can be independent of laxative misuse, and keeping a record of the latter separate from the former can be useful.

E = exercise

In the eating disorder diary, excessive exercise should be recorded with a simple tick/cross. Do not use this to record usual daytime activity such as walking to the bus stop. Rather you are attempting to keep a record of your abuse of exercise for pathological reasons. You will have a sense of whether your exercise is driven by these reasons or not.

Where you are completing an exercise diary, your primary problem will be compulsive over-exercise, such as in muscle dysmorphia. Here you should be recording a more detailed description of exercise, as noted above.

Thoughts

Here you should record the circumstances in which these behaviours were occurring. I reiterate that in this section your behaviour diary is acting like a pocket therapist. You can pour your heart out here and be brutally honest with yourself. You can write anything you wish, and even use it to try and make sense of complex feelings that may feel beyond words. Here is an honest example of someone doing 'all the wrong things':

> I woke up feeling so fat today. Yesterday was a dreadful day. I will do so much better today. I will try not to eat until lunchtime.
>
> I can't keep it up. By mid-morning I'm ravenous. I keep telling myself that I'll eat an apple, but I've ended having two burgers and chips. I feel so disgusted.
>
> Go to the gym and have a workout for two hours instead of lunch. Feel more 'in control'. Aim to eat nothing else today, but allow myself a glass of wine this evening.
>
> Ravenous, but still in control.
>
> Just had an argument with my boss. Feel like he can 'see through me'.
>
> At home I just keep on bingeing. I can't control myself. I feel like such a fat bastard. Make myself vomit afterwards, feel disgusted with myself. Plan to eat nothing tomorrow.

Feelings

In this section you can record the feelings associated with the description of thoughts given previously. Here is an example from someone with muscle dysmorphia:

> I feel much more in control today. Could almost convince myself I'm happy! At last I can do a workout and manage to stop after 20 minutes. Most people would think that was a failure, but for me it feels like freedom.
>
> Still hate what I see in the mirror. Can't bear to look at my legs. So spindly!

How do you use the diary?

Behaviour diaries like these are the cornerstones of treatment with therapists, and you may be using the diary in conjunction with the weekly input of a therapist. They will review the diary and help you to elucidate trends and patterns. If you are 'going it alone', nonetheless you could employ a similar process. Set aside time each week to review the diary. Ideally it should be for at least an hour, once a week, and at the same day/time. First thing in the morning at a weekend can be an ideal time. You are at your most reflective then, not distracted by what has happened in the day nor the trivial battles of the working week. Avoid constantly checking and rechecking past entries as you go along, but confine your review to these sessions.

There are three steps to the use of the diary. First, you record what is happening. Second, you review what is happening. Third, you change what is happening.

First steps: the initial two weeks

Remember that we talked of the diary as having two purposes: first, you are trying to work out what is going on; second, you are trying to change it. Begin by sticking to the first goal. Simply record things as and when they happen. Do not make too much effort to turn things around. The risk of trying to change things too early is that you will use your diary to deceive yourself. You will have a hidden motive to record inaccurate information. Allow yourself the 'luxury' of avoiding a battle with your illness. Simply write down what is happening in honest and neutral terms. Do this for two weeks.

Second steps: reviewing the situation

After two weeks you should read your diary in detail. You should have records of 14 days. If any days are missing, you need to ask yourself if this is the right time to attempt recovery.

At this stage, you may have a sense that something has gone wrong. For example, it is common to find that you increasingly fail to put any effort in whatsoever. You may develop quite extreme feelings about the food diary – regard it as a dreadful intrusion, or a waste of time, or deeply irritating, or very frightening. Think through what has gone right and what has gone wrong over the past two weeks.

At this stage you can also begin to spot trends. Are there certain days of the week when you are over-exercising? Is there any pattern to the days on which you are making yourself vomit more than others? What are the most typical triggers to binge eating? What has been your mood on days where you have eaten very little?

Patterns that emerge may be simple: for example, you may find that your eating is most disordered on the days when you have no breakfast. Patterns may also reflect deeper psychological issues. For example, you may find that compulsive exercise is far worse when you spend time with your parents. Sometimes the complex psychological issues merge with the simple patterns. When you begin to bridge the gap between the two, then you are almost becoming your own therapist.

Whether to weigh yourself?

Monitoring of weight is a complex issue, particularly for men with anorexia nervosa or bulimia, but also for some cases of muscle dysmorphia. Excessive self-weighing can be part of the problem, and it is easy to become obsessed about these matters. On the other hand, if you ignore your weight altogether you may find that what feels like an improvement is actually at the expense of weight loss.

Once you begin to alter your eating and exercise behaviours, you need to ensure that you are starting to put your feelings into words rather than behaviours. Monitoring your weight gives you a clue as to your success. Gross fluctuations in weight will suggest that behaviours are still present, though may be hidden from you.

If you have anorexia nervosa or bulimia, you should consider weighing yourself on a weekly basis. Decide when and where to do so and stick to this plan. Avoid the temptation to weigh yourself obsessively, or between your regular weekly weigh-ins. Most people find it best to weigh themselves when they wake up, and they can go about their daily business providing some distraction from thoughts of weight. Whilst fewer men than women with eating disorders are preoccupied with weight, nonetheless many men do experience some terror at the prospect of getting on the weighing scales.

For men with a propensity to over-exercise, and particularly men with muscle dysmorphia, an equivalent to excessive weighing can be 'mirror gazing'. Repetitively studying your body shape in the mirror can feed into behaviours, and is best avoided. It can be useful to record this in your behaviour diary.

Third steps: making behavioural changes – inoculating yourself

If you have an eating disorder, the principal goal is to stabilise your eating pattern and, in the case of anorexia nervosa, begin to achieve weight gain. Even if your problem is one of binge eating or overeating, the essence of an effective remedy is to plan three regular meals per day, with additional snacks between meals to prevent triggers of binge eating. For someone with anorexia nervosa this may feel overwhelming, and that is why many men with anorexia nervosa do eventually require professional help. Nonetheless, if you can take small steps to regularising your eating pattern, you will have won half the battle.

For men with bulimia nervosa, eating regular meals may feel counter-intuitive. After all, your problem is overeating, so surely you should be trying to eat less, not more? In reality, thrice daily mealtimes inoculate you against your eating disorder. It takes an edge off the highs and lows of satiety and hunger, the ultimate triggers of disordered eating.

To achieve this requires you to alter your relationship with food. To date, you will have tended to eat in response to feeling hungry or feeling full. However, if you have an eating disorder you can no longer trust these sensations. You have to approach food almost as if it is a medical pre-scription, rather than eating because your body is telling you to eat. This will not come naturally. To overcome these unnatural feelings, you will need to plan what you will eat in advance.

Planned regular meals are the core of successful behaviour therapy for an eating disorder. Here is a recent example from the food diary of one of my patients with bulimia nervosa:

7.15 am   Breakfast
10.00 am   Snack (fruit)
1.00 pm   Lunch (with others)
3.30 pm   Snack (cereal bar)
8.00 pm   Dinner (with family)

Be prepared that this will not go to plan. Men with eating disorders are programmed to see life as lurching between triumph and disaster. Rather than seeing a bad day as a disaster, try to learn from it.

In the example given above, the patient actually found himself bingeing at midnight. It was clear that he was eating an extremely calorifically restricted dinner, and thereby experiencing hunger in the middle of the night. By increasing the size of dinner and by introducing another snack before bedtime he was able to overcome this pattern. He did this for himself, without any instruction from me. So, the meal plan became:

7.15 am   Breakfast
10.00 am   Snack (fruit)
1.00 pm   Lunch (with others)
3.30 pm   Snack (cereal bar)
8.00 pm   Dinner (with family) – including dessert
10.00 pm   Cup of hot chocolate

Ideally you should avoid any risk of hunger or starvation. For many people this would involve ensuring *some form of calorific consumption every three hours*. Of course, everyone is different and, particularly if you are involved in considerable amounts of exercise, you may find you need to introduce snacks more frequently than this.

Again I would emphasise that you need to change your relationship with food and mealtimes. Regard mealtimes as a form of 'medical prescription'. If you were taking antibiotics or insulin several times a day, you would have no hesitation in putting aside time during a busy day for your medical treatment. In the same way, you need to prioritise meals, just as a diabetic would prioritise insulin injections. You may need to make changes to your life and its habits. You may need to consider how you will achieve this pattern in the context of your employment. Adjustments may be needed, strings pulled and miracles achieved! But the fundamental principle has to be that you are prioritising the treatment of your most serious medical condition over all else.

Most importantly, do not make excuses for yourself. There will be a part of you that wishes to list all the logical reasons why it is quite impossible to achieve regular mealtimes, but in your heart you will know that this is your illness speaking.

No surprises – meal planning

What you eat and when you eat it should not 'come out of the blue'. You should plan this in advance, and certainly the day before. Do not leave it to chance. If left to chance, your illness will take over and you will cheat. Here is an example of a meal planning record recently used by a man under my care:

7.00 am   Breakfast
11.00 am   Snack
1.00 pm   Lunch
4.00 pm   Snack
8.00 pm   Dinner
10.00 pm   Snack

Time	Description of food	How much	Place	S	B	V	L	E
7 am	Weetabix / full fat milk Black coffee Toast with low fat butter	Large bowl Small cup 2 – thin sliced	Kitchen					
11 am	Banana Orange juice	1 Small cup	Office					

1 pm	Tuna sandwich with low fat mayonnaise Ham sandwich – no butter Diet Coke	2 slices thick bread 1 can	Office			*	
4 pm	Apple and cereal bar	1	Office				*
8 pm	Pasta with cheese and ham sauce Yoghurt and banana Glass of wine	Large portion – large bowl 1 1 small	Kitchen			*	
10 pm	Hot chocolate and bourbon biscuit	1 mug	Bedroom				

Learning how to eat or exercise – overcoming dissociation

Many men with body image disorders have actually lost the skill of eating or exercising. Remember when it used to be fun? They may have learnt to exercise or eat in what is technically termed a dissociative (trance-like) state, where they are only half-aware of what they are doing. It can therefore be important to learn to eat in a slow methodical manner, in an unhurried and understood environment. Rather than trying to feel 'nothing' while you are exercising or eating, allow yourself to exercise or eat calmly, and become aware of what feelings you are experiencing during the process.

Do not distract yourself from your actions by eating breakfast in the car, eating dinner at the cinema or eating in such a hurry that you lose touch with those feelings. Try to avoid exercising to the soundtrack of pounding music that distracts you from yourself. You need to learn how to listen to your body again.

Aim to avoid temptation, not resist temptation

You will find it far easier to avoid temptation than to resist temptation. So ensure that any 'dangerous' foods are unavailable to you, and that food most readily available to you will be your planned meals. For example, if you plan to eat a slice of pizza, try to make sure that the larger pizza is not immediately available to you, lest it trigger a binge.

If you have anorexia nervosa you may have the opposite problem. However, in the same way you need to avoid rather than resist temptation. Make sure that the necessary quantities are there on your plate. As much as possible, measure those quantities out in advance. Keep up your battle with your anorexia nervosa until your plate is empty. If you have the means of disposing of food too easily, then undoubtedly you will succumb to temptation. Create a 'healing' environment around your mealtimes. Eating with your closest confidante, such as a parent, can be very useful.

If your problem is self-induced vomiting, then initially aim to lengthen the time between eating and vomiting episodes. For example, if you are eating with other people their presence may be useful in inhibiting your behaviour. If not, you might write down a clear strategy for things that you could do to stop vomiting after mealtimes. This might include phoning a friend, writing your thoughts and feelings down in a book, preparing your bag for tomorrow's work or playing the piano. Make it personal, clear and very direct.

Summary

Establishing healthy habits is more than just changing what you do. It requires you to think about why you are doing it, and how you are doing it. Keeping a behaviour diary is the most effective strategy. This must not only document behaviours, but also look at thoughts and feelings. Begin by simply recording what is happening. If you are unable to do even this, then it will be very hard for you to recover and you may need additional help. After you have been recording your behaviours for some time, you can start to try and change them. Where eating is an issue, this will involve meal planning. It will also involve simple, direct strategies for overcoming your usual reactions to mealtimes. Where exercise is an issue, planning your schedule in advance is also helpful. As well as thinking about what you should *not* be doing, think about replacing those behaviours or activities. The ability to accurately record your situation in a behaviour diary is the most fundamental step towards recovery. If you have done this, then you are well on the road to a better life. Well done!

Chapter 16

Stage 4: Thinking straight

This chapter is a practical guide to cognitive therapy, one of the most effective treatments. We look at the way people with muscle dysmorphia automatically think about themselves and their world. We examine the spontaneous distorted thoughts that men with eating disorders develop. These distorted thoughts are like the hardwiring of the brain. But your thoughts are within your control. You can literally learn to think straight by identifying and challenging the warped thinking:

Joe was one of the best students in his year. One of his strengths was his ability to organise himself. He would make a revision plan well in advance, and break it down into steps and stages. He kept an electronic diary where he classified all the things he had 'to do'. He classified his list into 'quick' and 'significant', and every morning he would update the list. That way he always felt 'on top of things'.

This was in complete contrast with his personal life. He put so much into his studies that he seemed to avoid thinking about all his personal problems. He had just 'been dumped' and his ex partner had started seeing this guy who was taller, slimmer and fitter than him. He couldn't admit to himself how upset he had been, and he decided that it had all come about because he was too fat.

He set himself the aim of not eating at all during daytime and only beginning to eat at dusk. He found he could manage this for a couple of days but then he couldn't maintain it, so started to binge always followed by vomiting. He called these days his 'fat days' and the other days his 'thin days'. The fat days seemed to prove to him that he was a total failure.

Meanwhile, other problems were starting to mount up. He had got himself into debt, buying a car he couldn't really afford and then failing to meet the repayments. His student loan seemed to grow and grow. He found he couldn't even pay simple bills like gas and electricity. He ignored letters from utility companies and the bank, just shoving them into the back of a drawer and forgetting about them. Of course no one realised this was going on. At college he was known as 'the organised one'.

Men who develop body image disorders often demonstrate what are termed cognitive distortions, exemplified above. The way they think about themselves, their world and their future becomes distorted, like software in a computer program going wonky. Luckily we have done considerable research on how to reprogram the computer, by challenging these cognitive distortions and helping people 'think straight'. This approach is known as cognitive therapy and is usually combined with behavioural therapy.

Cognitive therapy arises from hard science. For example, numerous studies of how people analyse their world demonstrate that humans have a propensity to prove their hunches or hypotheses true, rather than to prove them false. If you believe that you are fat, you will notice, assimilate and remember the few occasions when this idea of yourself seems proven by the outside world. You will completely ignore the 99 occasions when the opposite is proven.

As well as problems with the content of thoughts, many men with eating disorders get overwhelmed by problems, and this emotional 'can't cope' state triggers eating behaviours such as bingeing, vomiting, starvation or over-exercise. Men who develop body image disorders have been shown to have deficiencies in problem solving, as well as cognitive distortions.

For example, if Joe had applied the same level of organisation and structure to his personal life as his professional life, he would be able to overcome his difficulties and avoid allowing them to exacerbate his eating disorder. The contrast between Joe's rational, focused approach to his studies and the emotional, overwhelmed approach to his personal life, for example 'filing' overdue bills in the back of the drawer, is typical of many people with body image disorders.

In my therapy practice, I normally combine cognitive therapy with problem-solving therapy. Although they are both different approaches, they have a lot in common and it is often natural to deal with both issues at the same time. Learning to problem solve can be the first step towards recovery. Sometimes your problems are so numerous it is difficult to 'see the wood for the trees'. Sometimes you won't have properly defined your problem. It may lack focus and definition. For example, Joe was depressed because of the end of his relationship. He thought this was because he was too fat. He thought that by becoming thinner he would become more attractive. He was overwhelmed with his financial difficulties and preferred just to ignore them rather than tackle them.

Some of Joe's problems are easy to identify. If he had applied the same energy to tackling these problems as he applied at work, he could have easily begun to sort things out. 'Having the electricity cut off' and 'having his car repossessed' were both significant issues for which he could have found a quick solution. Why didn't he? The emotional implications of these issues overwhelmed Joe. He had expectations of driving a good car, and to abandon those expectations would have threatened his pride. He was so used to regarding himself as 'organised' that the overdue electricity bill was more than just a debt – it represented a real threat to his sense of identity. These deeper rooted beliefs about himself are sometimes termed schemata and we often examine them in a powerful variant of cognitive therapy known as schema-focused therapy. One such schema is known as the *perfectible self*.

However, some of Joe's problems were less well-defined and with less obvious solutions. For example, he was broken hearted. Grief is a healthy and natural emotion. But Joe wasn't able to grieve naturally, by sitting and feeling upset, by putting his feeling into words or even by allowing himself to be aware of his feelings. For most men with body image disorders, emotions aren't the problem but rather their ability to tolerate them and express them in words rather than behaviours. Joe's eating disorder was triggered by emotions of which he had only a vague awareness.

Problem solving the RASCAL way

To help people like Joe learn to problem solve, we developed something called the RASCAL approach to problem solving. This describes stages of:

- **R**eview
- **A**nalyse
- **S**olve
- **C**ost
- **A**ct
- **L**earn

It isn't rocket science – just a basic way of analysing things. Think up your own system if you like – the main thing is to *have* a system. The RASCAL approach has been adopted by others, not because it is the work of genius but because it is simple and memorable. When it comes to problem solving, keeping it simple is essential.

RASCAL stands for six stages in the process: you *Review* the situation; you *Analyse* the problems; you look for *Solutions*; you weigh up the pros and the cons in a *Cost-benefit analysis*; you then *Act* on your analysis by putting your solutions into practice; and finally you *Learn* from the whole process. Of all of these stages, it is the Act stage that people struggle with most of all. Often it is better to take the wrong action and then learn from it than be frozen in indecision.

Review

Sit down with a blank sheet of paper and review your problems. Write them down as specifically as possible. For example, instead of Joe writing 'I can't control my eating', or 'I have money problems', he would be specifying 'I can't stop myself from bingeing and vomiting', 'my car is about to be repossessed and the electricity disconnected'.

Making a very clear problem list is important, and sometimes people mix up all sorts of interrelated problems. Clearly defining and separating the issues is important, but it may take several sheets of paper. Don't be worried if you write too much or if you need to go back and make lots of changes. I often find that it is only by the tenth item in the list, or the second draft, that you are really getting to the core of what is going on.

Analyse

Your list may be very big by now. That doesn't matter. Try to categorise the problems into some sort of order. First, you may have listed problems for which there will not be solutions. In Joe's case, he still loved his ex-partner, but no amount of problem solving would address that issue. His real problem wasn't that the relationship had ended, but that he didn't know how to cope.

Next, focus on problems over which you might have some control. List them in two separate hierarchies. Which are the problems that can be dealt with quickly and which are slower? Which are the problems that are most significant and which are least significant? You might be left with four lists: significant and quick; significant and slow; not significant and quick; not significant and slow. Use any approach you like, but try and analyse your list of problems so it gives you some sense of priority and helps you avoid feeling overwhelmed. It is that sense of being overwhelmed that precipitates body image disorders, just as some people want to pull the bedcovers over their heads and hope the world will go away.

Solve

For each problem, brainstorm a range of possible answers. Let your creative juices flow! Let your imagination run riot. Don't be frightened of the absurd. The longer the list of solutions, the better able you will be to whittle it down to the correct one. For example:

> Joe notes that his body image disorder is particularly bad at the weekend, compared to his working week. The structure and routine of lectures from Monday to Friday is lost at the weekend. He thinks of ways he might give his Saturdays more structure. He writes down five ideas: visit my sister in

Oxford, go fishing with Dan, join the archery club, do the laundry, get a weekend job.

Cost

Start to think through the pros and cons of each of your solutions. Shut your eyes and imagine the reality of each option. Will it work? Is it feasible? For example:

Joe has such a difficult relationship with his sister that visiting her will not help at all, and his idea stems from a fantasy of 'playing happy families', rather than the reality of the arguments into which they will descend.

Doing the laundry is sensible and achievable, freeing him up later in the day. But he does not want to make this his only solution, as it won't fill much time, it seems a little bit boring and he will probably just sit there gloomily introspecting.

Getting a weekend job sounds reasonable at first glance, as it would also help his cash-flow problem. But when he thinks of the reality, he knows that 'weekend job' really means 'bar work' in his town. That would just encourage him to drink more and he'd end up getting to bed really late, probably after a midnight 'binge'.

'Going fishing with his friend' and 'taking up archery' seem like really attractive options and will give him a bit of distraction from himself.

Act

Sometimes it is better to do than think. Some people become so mired in introspection that they are unable to take decisive action. The combination of feeling emotionally overwhelmed by your problems and being indecisive in acting on them is often at the root of poor problem solving skills. If you act, and things go wrong, you can then use this as a learning experience. If you do not act, you will never learn. For example:

Joe joined the archery club and turns up on the first day, but it is hideous. Everyone seems to know each other, and no one bothers to talk to him. He doesn't have a clue what he is doing, and it just feels like that horrible time when he started a new school and was too shy to talk to anyone. After 20 minutes, he has had enough and decides to leave.

At first glance this plan would appear to have been a total failure. In fact Joe is able to learn some important principles from this. He discovers he is a much shyer person than he had realised, but is also good at covering it up. He needs more structured activity, and more familiarity. He doesn't deal well with strangers or strange situations.

Action is critical to problem solving. It is easier to try, than to prove it can't be done.

Learn

Having tried out a range of solutions to a range of problems, review your original list. Don't wait for a week to have passed before reviewing things. By then, your memory will have distorted the process. Don't review things instantly either; you won't be able to see the wood for the trees. Focus not so much on the problem and its solution, but on the process of what actually happened. Learn from the process more than the event. For example:

> Joe decides to tackle his bills by ringing up the gas company. He ends up being connected to a call centre in another country. He gets very exasperated and starts to shout down the phone when he struggles to make himself understood. The person at the other end puts the phone down in him. Another disaster!
>
> He looks at the process, and decides that he might have better dealt with things in writing. In any case, the amount of money owed to the gas board is so small that he could simply have added the debt to his banking debts, and consolidated the debts in a single place.
>
> The interest rates from the bank loan are far lower than the potential fines from the gas company. He makes an appointment at the bank, and it goes really well. He realises that half the problem was his failure to answer letters or communicate with the bank in any way. Once he is speaking to someone face to face, they make him realise he'll actually be saving money by getting a low interest loan and paying it off gradually. He will have to give up his car, but if he does that he should have no more debts at all within four months.
>
> Joe ended up fishing with his friend. They left early in the morning, well before dawn, and had a really good time, even though they didn't catch anything. Afterwards, his friend suggested they have brunch together. He felt very uncomfortable at this but forced himself to do it, choosing a healthy option. He wanted to make himself feel sick afterwards, but resisted the urge and felt really pleased with himself. Afterwards he suggested they go to the new James Bond movie that evening. He had been planning to get really drunk that night, but knew that whenever he drank too much he would end up bingeing and vomiting afterwards. The film ended early, and his mate wanted

to go on to a party, but Joe decided to go home early and get a good night's sleep. The next day he woke up feeling happy, relaxed and calm. He hadn't slept so well in weeks.

Joe already demonstrated good problem-solving skills, but had only applied them to his studies. Problem solving the RASCAL way has been trialled in many different situations. We have found that problem solving helps not only men with body image disorders, but also people with a range of addictions and related self-damaging behaviours. There isn't scope to detail every aspect of problem solving – that would take a whole book – but the principle behind the RASCAL approach is that problem solving isn't a natural talent. It is something you can learn and should practise. The more you do it, the better you get. Eventually it becomes a state of mind. There is good evidence that high achievers have exceptional problem-solving skills.

Eventually you won't need pen and paper. Your brain will start to think in this way without any effort. However, when you start to tackle the triggers of your body image disorder by problem solving the RASCAL way, it is best to write things down. Let the process of problem solving become part of the process of keeping the behavioural diary described earlier.

Changing minds, changing thoughts

Men with body image disorders have been shown to develop fixed, rigid and inaccurate thoughts about themselves, which are technically termed cognitive distortions. Sometimes the system of thought becomes deeply embedded, and these systems are known as schemata. There is substantial evidence that irrational automatic thoughts maintain the body image disorders, and also evidence that understanding these thoughts and changing them can substantially improve the eating disorder itself.

It is not always necessary to understand the origin of the thoughts in order to change the pattern, although this can sometimes help. For example, sometimes conflicts and problems in childhood have created a brain that is hardwired to produce thoughts associated with low self-esteem and perfectionism. Understanding these childhood influences can be helpful in some cases, but it isn't always essential. In all cases, it is necessary to deal with the here and now before delving more deeply.

A bit of science

Wason's Four-card Trick

In 1966, Wason created a study of how humans apply logic. Students were given four cards laid out in a row and informed that all cards had a letter on one side and a number on the other. They appeared like this:

They were told: 'Whenever there is a vowel on one side of a card, there is an even number on the other.' They were then asked to name the minimum cards needed to be viewed, to see if that rule was correct or false. Virtually all the students chose the E, but very few chose the 7. This has been repeated in many different ways and the results are consistent. From this, we can conclude that people are naturally disposed to prove their hypotheses true, not to prove them false. Thus we can understand a great deal of human nature.

For instance, if I believe that all women are bad drivers, I will pay selective attention to every single 'bad woman driver' and ignore the many good women drivers. If I believe I am fat or ugly, I will seek confirmation of this by paying greater attention to comments that confirm this, yet ignore comments that refute it. I will even remember these events with greater clarity.

The story is slightly more complicated than I have presented. Studies using much more relevant situations than cards with numbers and letters suggest that we are slightly better at applying logic where necessary. What seems to be the case is that we have two stages of thinking: first, we look at the relevance of the task; second, we apply logic to the situation. What is certainly the case is that humans are not logical in the way we think. Our thoughts are full of prejudices, assumptions and unsupported judgements. Men with body image disorders apply those prejudices to themselves. We pay selective attention to situations or events that support our pre-existing prejudices, rather than testing them out in a neutral and dispassionate way. The essence of cognitive behaviour therapy is to make the patient a 'scientist' – to help them identify possible errors in their thinking and then put them to the test.

Thoughts and feelings about yourself become entwined with thoughts about body image. Consider the following statement:

> The guys never asked me out for a drink with them tonight. They didn't ask me because they think I'm fat. That's because I binged yesterday and it shows that I am a fat, awful person. I'll never be popular.

It would be logical to explore the many reasons why you weren't asked out for a drink. You weren't around when it was organised. They think you're teetotal. They forgot. They feel threatened by your immense talent and charm. They wanted to organise a birthday party for you. They hate you. Then you would explore the evidence in favour of each proposition, and work out the most likely explanation. Then you might put it to the test – most obviously by asking someone. However, the statement betrays how someone with a body image disorder really thinks. How can 'the guys' know that you binged yesterday? How could a single binge have any meaningful impact on appearance? Why would 'the guys' be bothered? Finally, why would a temporary binge result in permanent unpopularity?

Your thoughts mingle with beliefs about yourself, your world and your future. The role of cognitive therapy is to make you a scientist – better able to apply logic and, particularly, to identify cognitive distortions. MAD-POMS is the framework we have developed to help people remember the various cognitive distortions.

Cognitive therapy – the MAD-POMS way

MAD-POMS is simply an acronym to remember some of the common errors of reasoning that we see in men with body image disorders. See if you can apply any of these examples to yourself.

Magnification

A small problem is taken out of all proportion:

I didn't binge all week, and then suddenly yesterday was terrible. I'll never be able to stop myself bingeing. It's just going on and on and on.

Arbitrary inference

Arbitrary inference refers to unjustified conclusions. For example:

She ignored me all day today. She thinks I'm a wimp. I just need to go to the gym.

Dichotomous thinking

Here you think in 'black and white'. If everything isn't wonderful then it must be terrible:

I took the doctor's advice and tried to gain weight, but I just can't do it. I might as well give up completely.

Personalisation

You take a wholly neutral event and apply it to yourself in an overpersonal way:

My secretary never offered me biscuits with my coffee, even though everyone else got them. She thinks I'm fat.

Over-generalisation

A very specific, limited event gets applied far beyond its true relevance:

I binge because I am a completely useless person. I have no control over anything in my life. Nothing I do will ever be right.

Minimisation

This is the opposite of magnification. A major positive event is treated as if inconsequential:

Everyone was laughing at my joke. I think they only laughed at my jokes because they felt so sorry for me.

Selective abstraction

You take a highly specific event, in this case the physical characteristics of a woman's ex-partner, and abstract it into having more meaning than it really holds – in this case the tastes of the woman concerned:

Her last boyfriend was 6 ft. She would only find tall, skinny men attractive.

MAD-POMS system

The MAD-POMS system is a framework for examining how people's brains become hardwired to create self-defeating thoughts about themselves. Can you recognise any of these in yourself? From countless research studies, we know that cognitive distortions are involved in supporting and sustaining many aspects of body image disorders, including the behaviours, low self-esteem and perfectionism that so often lie at the root.

Cognitive therapy involves identifying and recognising these irrational thoughts and then testing them out. When carried out with a therapist this approach is known as *collaborative empiricism*. You collaborate with your therapist in an experiment. Rather than simply having a therapist tell you that you're talking nonsense, you put it to the test and consider alternative explanations by means of dialectic or discussion.

We have found problem solving and behaviour therapy to be highly effective as a form of self-help. Cognitive therapy tends to works at its best

Table 16.1 Cognitive distortions and counter-arguments

Cognitive distortion	Counter-argument
I've tried to stop using laxatives for three weeks now and it hasn't made any difference at all.	I have actually reduced my laxative intake by 10 per cent, which isn't too bad after three years of persistent use. I always want instant results, but I need to learn to slow down a bit.
No one is going to find me attractive when I look like a stick insect. I really need to build the muscles in my legs and steroids will do the job quickly.	People come in all shapes and sizes and I'm no different to anyone else. Taking steroids isn't exactly the sexiest thing in the world.

when you collaborate with a trained therapist. However, it is possible to do some of the work on your own.

Take a piece of paper and fold it down the middle. On the left-hand side, write down at least five examples of cognitive distortions you have recently used on yourself, using the MAD-POMS system as an aide-memoire. Then put your pen down. Go and do something else for at least five minutes. Next sit down at the table and examine the list. On the right-hand side of the list, write down counter-arguments. If you can't think of any counter-arguments, try to imagine what a friend or relative might be saying. Table 16.1 shows some examples.

If you regularly build identification of cognitive distortions into your diary, you will begin to scrape away at the very essence of your body image disorder. If the bricks of that disorder are your behaviours, then the cement is your cognitive distortions.

Summary

Men with body image disorders wrongly believe that thoughts are beyond their control. Far from it. You can decide what attitude to take. You can learn to problem solve. If you train yourself to think positively, analyse rationally and seek appropriate explanations when things go wrong, you can begin to break down the body image disorder. Men with body image disorders tend to think irrationally. They are easily overwhelmed by problems and put blame for problems squarely on their own shoulders. If you practise the techniques in this module, you can begin to think straight.

Chapter 17

Stage 5: Feeling good

The core to the successful treatments of muscle dysmorphia, eating disorders and compulsive over-exercise is as simple as ABC. In Stages 3 and 4, you explored the behaviours and the cognitions. In this stage you examine your 'affect'. Affect is the word psychiatrists and psychologists use to describe someone's emotions. Tackling emotions, thoughts and behaviours is known to be the best way to overcome your problems. In this chapter, we look at how past traumas may have caused current feelings. We explore the process of anger management and dealing with conflict. Finally, we look at the issue of low self-esteem.

Once your behaviours and thoughts have been modified, most people automatically return to a sense of well-being. You feel competent again. Instead of being controlled by your eating disorder or exercise compulsion, you are now in charge. 'Good feelings' arise spontaneously from this state of autonomy. Now you find your sense of well-being has huge effects. Restoration of optimism makes you positive in your outlook and your self-esteem returns. With self-confidence and self-esteem, you like yourself: hence the world likes you. Studies of highly successful people have demonstrated this 'optimism' as a key feature. Optimists are more likely to employ the analytic process of problem solving (the RASCAL way) I described in Chapter 16. They imagine their future, and so are better able to achieve their dreams by breaking them down into a series of specific goals. You have a tremendous ability to generate this state of mind. Too many people believe that their emotional state is dependent on factors beyond their control. Instead, it is an attitude of mind, and you are in the driver's seat.

While the causes of an eating disorder or body image problem may arise from factors beyond the more immediate behaviours and thoughts, for some people it is not necessary to delve into the past in order to make these changes. Nonetheless, an important minority does require additional work in these areas. The abnormal behaviours of your eating disorder or exercise compulsion have been used to keep these feelings at arm's length. It has been described to me as being 'cocooned' by the eating disorder. When the cocoon is removed, old and bad memories come back. The following is written for the minority who may feel overwhelmed by these memories.

Scars and traumas

Most men with body image disorders have experienced a happy and nurturing childhood. However, a minority will have been denied consistent love and others may have even experienced physical or sexual abuse. A single one-off trauma in childhood, however severe, is rarely the cause of adult distress. More commonly it is the repeated trauma that gets under your skin as a child and starts to change the way you think about things.

Physical abuse in childhood can make a child persistently anxious and on the alert. This has been termed 'frozen watchfulness'. This state can remain with you into adulthood. For many boys, the result is a tremendous sense of anger. This may cause episodic bouts of uncontrolled rage as an adult. The boy clenches his fists and bites his tongue as he is beaten. The man hits out at real or even imagined attacks. There can be interchangeability in the eating behaviours, exercise compulsions and other behaviours that help to neutralise these feelings. Getting into fights, getting drunk or cutting yourself become ways of neutralising the residual feelings.

Much the same applies to sexual abuse in childhood. Sexual abuse is common in men, yet so less frequently discussed than in women. It may have involved threats and force, or it may have been the result of bribes or persuasion that leave complex feelings behind as an adult. Sexual abuse of boys does not just refer to obvious sexual activity. It can include being forced to watch sexual activity or porn films. One of the hardest things to come to terms with is your response to this. You may have felt disgusted at the time, but it is very common during a sexual assault to experience some form of sexual response such as an erection or ejaculation. Sometimes the abuser will have made sure this happens. It does not alter the reality of the sexual abuse, but it creates the horrendous cocktail of self-blame and shame that can haunt you throughout your life.

Men and women are both known to abuse boys. The gender of your assailant can create further complexities. Abuse by a woman is deeply traumatic, but society has often employed a double standard to these events, portraying it as some sort of initiation into adulthood. While the scars run deep throughout your life, it becomes hard to talk about these things for fear of them being dismissed or trivialised. Abuse by a man, or older boy, can create lifelong confusion over sexual orientation. Abuse within families can rip the life and soul out of the family, denying you your rightful childhood. There are three stages in beginning to come to terms with this. First, it is important to recognise that you have been abused, even if you didn't scream or fight. Second, it is important to recognise that you are not to blame. Third, it is important to become a survivor and not a victim.

It can be very hard to address these problems all on your own. These paragraphs have been designed not as a comprehensive guide, but as an initial stepping stone. Many people find it helpful to begin to write down their life story, as the first step to making sense of things. The next step is to seek professional help through counselling services. Good counselling focuses on the here and now as much as the past. Persistent reiteration of the past without addressing the future can embed you in victimhood. You cannot change your past, but you can break the cycle of abuse and lay the ghosts to rest.

Dealing with anger

Many men with body image disorders have problems in dealing with anger. Sometimes they are incapable of giving direct expression to their anger, and so are left expressing it through their self-destructive behaviours. Sometimes the rage is suppressed, but then bursts forth inappropriately and without focus. Anger is a tremendously positive force in your life. Learning to channel your anger into creative outlets can transform you. Anger management is the therapy by which many men learn these techniques. You may wish to consider an anger management course, and information on this may be available from your local doctor or library. The essence of successful anger management is first to identify the triggers and second to learn to put your feelings into words instead of behaviours. It is not your right to be angry with someone and then punch them, or to hurt yourself. In this way you are conquered by your anger. It is your right to be angry with someone and to explain why. In this way you conquer your anger.

Dealing with people

Many men with body image disorders have additional relationship problems. As your behaviours change, your relationship with yourself will change. As your relationship with yourself changes, your relationship with other people will change. In my private practice, much time is spent in managing eating disorders and exercise compulsions by means of couple therapy or family therapy. A form of psychotherapy known as interpersonal therapy is also extremely helpful in some cases of eating disorders. Even without formal therapy, it is possible to recognise the need to change relationships, or change your attitude to relationships. For some men with body image disorders, this is the sine qua non, necessary and sufficient, to maintain recovery.

Self-esteem

Self-esteem issues can arise not only from the extremes of sexual abuse, but from persistent erosion of self-worth. Your illness in itself may be the major contributing factor, and your self-esteem may be restored by your ability to change your behaviours. However, issues of self-esteem can arise from how you have been treated by your parents, or from bullying at school. There is a vast academic literature on the effects of the former, particularly in eating disorders. Where your mother or father has made their love entirely conditional on either how they are feeling or what you have achieved, this creates a situation in which you are dependent on others for your own sense of self-worth in adulthood. The happy, stable adult will have been the recipient of unconditional parental love. Conditional love may generate low self-esteem in adulthood. However, in clinical practice I have become increasingly aware of the impact of bullying. You may have had the loveliest of homes, with doting and caring parents, but persistent bullying at school, particularly in the teenage years, robs you of self-confidence. More than 50 per cent of the men I have treated in clinical practice have been the victims of bullying, and often are too ashamed to discuss it even 20 years after the events. They are haunted by the experiences and remain changed by them. Very often the bullying has been entirely random. Teenagers are like little Nietzschean Nazis, choosing their victims at random so as not to be the victim themselves. Allow yourself to speak of these matters as the first step towards change.

On occasion, self-esteem is so low that it creates a disorder of anxiety or depression. Whereas transient melancholy is common in the early stages of recovery from a body image problem, it becomes abnormal if you are feeling low on most days of the week for at least two weeks. Where your low mood starts to interfere with your ability to take care of yourself, or even generates thoughts that life is not worth living, it may be that you are developing a depressive illness, and must seek medical help.

Conclusion

Recovery from a body image disorder usually brings a sense of restored well-being and optimism. Once you start to respect yourself, the world starts to respect you more. All the pieces come together at the same time and, almost without realising it, you wake up one day and realise you might even be happy.

For some people, past traumas may continue to haunt them. Learning to deal with feelings through subsequent therapy can be helpful. Interpersonal therapy, couple and family therapies can be particularly potent. Anger management is also very useful. Where there have been issues of abuse, the chance to speak to a wise counsellor can be invaluable.

Chapter 18

Stage 6: Seeking professional help

A consumer's guide

We have already seen that men with eating disorders will have very mixed feelings about getting better. The decision to seek professional help is therefore a defining moment, even if you still feel ambiguous. That first consultation with a professional can be a 'make or break' situation. A number of studies concerning men with eating disorders have shown that professionals' attitudes can either boost or undermine your intentions.

Role of the family doctor

Most men or boys with eating disorders will approach a family doctor (general practitioner) as the first port of call. Family doctors have a primary responsibility for identification of eating disorders, as well as early management of risk, physical examination and co-ordination of treatment. The family doctor therefore has a critical role in your treatment. How this can operate is explored in the following stories:

> Chris had been making himself sick to control his weight for the past three years. At first this was associated with binge eating, but later he carried on making himself sick even when he restricted his diet. As a result, his weight had fallen fairly dramatically, and his mum had asked him what was wrong. He denied everything. Things came to a head when he noticed some blood in his vomit. He became very worried that he had a potentially fatal problem, and decided to see his GP. He had never needed to consult with the family doctor before, so he didn't really know what to expect. He found it very off-putting. It was quite difficult to make an appointment in the first place, and then when he saw his GP he didn't know what to say. His family doctor was an old bloke in a pinstripe suit with half-moon glasses, and he seemed a bit out of touch.
>
> Chris wished he had written things down on a piece of paper before seeing the doctor, and everything just poured out in a rather chaotic manner. The family doctor only had four minutes for the appointment, the surgery was

busy, but he actually listened very carefully, didn't say too much, and asked some really helpful questions about the way Chris felt about his body, his unhappiness at school and his relationship with his mum.

His GP was fairly honest in admitting that he did not know much about eating disorders, and there certainly wasn't time to deal with everything in such a short appointment. He suggested they meet again for a longer chat at the end of the surgery a few days later. Chris had no hesitation in agreeing. Chris had been particularly impressed by the way his GP had firstly seemed to have a genuine desire to understand, and secondly had been honest enough about his own lack of knowledge.

The second time they met they had half an hour to talk things through, and the GP did a thorough physical examination. He arranged some blood tests. The third time they met, his GP was able to state that there was nothing immediately worrying about his physical health, but he confirmed what Chris already knew, namely that he was suffering from anorexia nervosa. He admitted that there was not much in the way of local services available for people with eating disorders, but he promised to see what could be done, if that was what Chris wanted.

Unfortunately the next time they were due to meet, Chris failed to turn up. Chris had decided that he could probably get better on his own, and didn't need professional help. He was reassured by the absence of immediate physical risk but was frightened that treatment would require him to gain weight, and that was something he simply could not tolerate. For the next year, Chris 'went to ground'. He tried to pretend to himself, and to others, that there was nothing really wrong any more. During that time his weight continued to fall until, as his mother put it 'you are just a skeleton'.

He decided to seek help again. Because his GP had been so surprisingly sympathetic and understanding, he had few fears in making another appointment. It felt good to be seeing a doctor who had seen him already, who could get a sense of the unfolding narrative, rather than just taking a 'snapshot' of the problem. He had liked the fact that his family doctor had listened to him. It felt like they could work together to tackle the problem, and that is exactly what happened.

Unfortunately the following can also occur:

Tony was in his thirties by the time he decided to talk to his doctor about his battle with bulimia. However, the battle had really been going on since he was 16 years old. It made him feel physically weak, but also he felt 'less of a man' because he had a problem that he wrongly perceived as being mainly a problem for women.

He had a busy job as a financial advisor, and so it was very difficult to get time off to see the doctor in any case. In the two days leading up to the appointment, his bulimia had really got out of hand. He had been bingeing and vomiting at least three times a day, and was feeling faint and dizzy every time he rose from his chair. When he saw his doctor, the appointment was delayed by over two hours, and he was concerned that he would not get back to work in time in the afternoon.

His doctor was a young woman who looked more nervous than he. She never looked up from her desk, but just seemed to be scribbling notes all the time. She asked him what the problem was, and he told her that he thought he might have an eating disorder. She was silent for a long time after that, and almost seemed embarrassed. Then she said: 'I don't think so. People with eating disorders are underweight, and if anything you are a little bit too plump. Anyway men aren't really at risk from eating disorders.'

Tony felt mortified at everything she had said. Irrational thoughts kept flashing into his mind. 'If I do have an eating disorder, but only women get eating disorders, then does that mean that I am gay? She is telling me that I look fat and that is exactly what I think too.'

Before he had a chance to reply, she then began to launch into all sorts of questions about his mood. She suggested to him that the real problem was stress relating to his work. She prescribed him an antidepressant tablet and asked him to come back eight weeks later. He didn't take the tablets and never returned. It took him another five years to pluck up the courage to see another doctor and thence was referred to a clinic. By then, the misconceptions about his illness that his family doctor displayed were deeply embedded in his own mind, and it took several years of therapy to overcome the damage.

Studies carried out by Beat, the UK eating disorder association, have shown that men with eating disorders sometimes experience situations like the latter. It is hard for family doctors to know everything, so a limited knowledge of eating disorders is understandable. It is far easier to have confidence in a doctor who is confident enough to admit what they know, and what they don't know. However, some doctors and nurses can hide their ignorance behind a professional veneer. The misconception that men do not suffer eating disorders pervades some health-care professionals, and indeed is one of the reasons why I wrote *The Invisible Man*.

None of this should put you off seeking help. However, what you should do is be prepared to shop around. Family doctors often work together in group practices and it is quite possible to find one family doctor who has particular expertise in, say, asthma and diabetes, and another who is more confident in dealing with issues of mental health. You can always be up front and tell the receptionist you want an appointment to talk about emotional difficulties. Often they would be able to guide you to the right person. Because family doctors are so busy, and average appointments in the UK are so brief, it can be very helpful to talk to a practice nurse, who may have more time. The gender of the family doctor may be relevant. You may be particularly embarrassed to be talking to another bloke, but you may be equally embarrassed to be chatting to a woman. On the other hand, research carried out by Beat suggested that gender is not nearly as important as finding someone who is understanding and empathic.

At best, your family doctor can offer you the opportunity to receive a proper diagnosis of your condition. They might carry out a physical examination, and normally additional blood tests, to establish any medical complications resulting from your eating disorder. Some eating disorders may even be managed within the family doctor's practice, sometimes through a practice nurse, a nurse specialising in mental health attached to the practice, or psychological counselling services. In other instances, the family doctor may suggest a referral to an eating disorder specialist for further therapy.

Navigating your way through the bureaucracy

Mental health services can seem quite fragmented with lots of different types of professionals and lots of different types of services. Unfortunately, in the UK over almost half the country does not have formal access to eating disorder services. Therefore treatments are carried out by general psychiatric services, or else require a referral to another geographical area. Eating disorder services can be oversubscribed, and may therefore be rationed or have long waiting lists.

Understanding the mental health team

You may be referred to a mental health team. The various people who contribute to such a team can have quite confusing titles. A psychiatrist is a medical doctor with special training in mental illnesses. Eating disorder specialists who are psychiatrists will have received particular training in psychotherapies, but also the various aspects of physical health, including nutrition. They would usually be responsible for prescribing medication, where appropriate. Eating disorder specialists who are clinical psychologists have particular expertise in psychological treatments. They may offer therapy over several sessions to talk through problems and find ways of solving them. Occupational therapists help people develop strategies for improving activities of daily living and help them to regain their self-confidence. Within eating disorder teams, occupational therapists will often provide quite specialist treatments, including creative therapies. They may also assist you in looking at practical aspects of your illness, such as shopping or dealing with exercise. Nurses are the backbone of a successful mental health team. Within eating disorder teams, nurses will have gained particular expertise in psychotherapies and also share with the doctors an ability to judge physical risk. Dieticians are rarely available within general mental health teams, but are common in eating disorder services. The best dieticians are not only able to impart their enhancement knowledge about nutrition, but can also convey that knowledge in a form that motivates and incentivises the patient. Specific teams may also include other specialists such as health support workers, art therapists, psychotherapists and family therapists.

When I look back at the many and varied services in which I have worked, it has rarely been an individual's discipline that has been as important as their personal qualities. Among the top ten eating disorder specialists of my acquaintance have been nurses, psychiatrists, psychologists, occupational therapists, psychotherapists and dieticians.

Self-help groups

One way of understanding the local bureaucracy is through local self-help groups. Attending a self-help group puts you in touch with other people who have experienced similar difficulties. You might learn informally which family doctors are most sympathetic towards people with eating disorders. You may hear the ins and outs of different specialist eating disorder services and how to access them. In the UK, the Beat provides a list of self-help groups by location on their website (www.b-eat.co.uk). The website also includes a list of statutory organisations providing treatment for eating disorders and there is additional helpful advice specifically for men with eating disorders. Most countries in the industrialised world have equivalent umbrella organisations, and the strength of this approach is that you become an informed consumer of the health care available. The following is a highly personal view of what you should be looking for, and what you should be avoiding, in whichever therapist you see.

Qualities of a good therapist

There are many different forms of therapy for eating disorders. At the end of the day, however, you need someone who will show you empathy and respect. Empathy is different to sympathy. Some good therapists can be quite challenging, and rightly so. Therapy isn't about having a shoulder to cry on. It is about someone who can engender change. Given the many different philosophies behind therapy, some therapists can become quite dedicated to one limited model of treatment. Far better is the therapist who can work flexibly, and draw on different philosophies of treatment according to their patient's need.

In the field of body image disorders, it is best to avoid therapists who employ unifactorial dogma. For example, some people with eating disorders will have experienced past traumas, but a bad therapist would perceive every person with an eating disorder to have suffered trauma, and therefore see the role of therapy as uncovering the trauma. There is increasing evidence that genetic factors are relevant, but a weak doctor would treat eating disorders as purely biological. As we have seen, conflicts in the family may be relevant, but a simplistic family therapist might 'blame the mother'. Your therapist needs to work flexibly towards finding the right solution for you, rather than inflexibly imposing their own theoretical dogma.

Most people with eating disorders are highly intelligent and well read. Many have formed a deep and detailed understanding of their own condition by the time they seek professional help. It is therefore important that the therapist is not merely there to provide you with facts, but to motivate and instil hope. What you need is someone who will inspire you towards change.

Finally, what all effective treatments have in common is a joint emphasis on both thoughts/feelings and behaviours. Therapy that simply addresses behaviours tends not to produce lasting change. Equally limited is therapy that does not require any behavioural change. In anorexia nervosa, weight gain is the fuel of psychotherapy. In bulimia nervosa, cessation of the binge–purge cycle allows you to address the underlying cognitive schemata. Continued over-exercising during therapy for muscle dysmorphia renders that psychotherapy a sterile intellectual exercise.

Different forms of therapy

There is not space in this book to describe in detail all the various forms of therapy that may be available for your eating disorder. If you have very severe physical symptoms, such as very low weight or abnormal blood results, it may be necessary for you to receive medical treatment before therapy can commence. Ultimately you are likely to be offered some form of 'talking therapy'. Various different types of talking therapy are described in the National Institute for Clinical Excellence (NICE) guidelines, and these can be accessed free via the NICE website (www.nice.org.uk). Different versions of talking therapy include cognitive behavioural therapy (CBT), a variant form of CBT known as mindfulness CBT, cognitive analytic therapy, psychodynamic psychotherapy, group therapy, interpersonal therapy, motivation enhancement therapy and family therapy.

For some people with eating disorders, creative therapy such as art therapy, music therapy and psychodrama can be very helpful, particularly when your immediate feelings are beyond words. It is important that you understand the rationale for the type of therapy that you are offered, and you should feel free to discuss and even challenge the approach suggested by health care professionals.

Sometimes, it is appropriate to suggest medication (tablets) in addition to psychotherapy. For example, many people with body image problems also suffer from depression, and the level of depression can be a barrier to being able to work in psychotherapy. It is therefore appropriate for this to be suggested. Likewise, some men with bulimia nervosa, binge eating or muscle dysmorphia are known to benefit from particular types of medication. However, I recently published an article in *Evidence Based Medicine* arguing that medication alone was not the best approach, even though it may seem like the simplest solution for both family doctors and their patients. People whose body image disorders improve with medication alone have a higher risk of relapse than those who also receive some form of psychotherapy. In essence, psychotherapy assists you in understanding your own condition. The thoughts and feelings that lie beneath the surface in body image disorders can re-emerge years later. Psychotherapy is better able to assist in relapse prevention. Insight and autonomy are the cornerstones to a lasting recovery.

You should receive a treatment that fits the best available evidence for your condition. Even in areas lacking specialist services, there are usually formal arrangements to access treatment outside of your area. Many specialists will accept referrals from all over the country. If you have difficulty accessing treatment, it is your right to seek an explanation. It is a sad fact that accessing specialist services appears more difficult for men than for women. In the UK, you can contact the Patient Advice and Liaison Service (PALS) in your area and they can act as your advocate, giving you assistance in resolving such disputes. Most industrialised countries will have similar patient advocacy services. It can be helpful to know your rights.

Different modes of therapy

Outpatients

Therapy for eating disorders is usually provided on an outpatient basis for mild and moderate cases. The advantage of outpatient treatment is that you can often fit treatment around your everyday normal routine. This means that, as your eating disorder improves, so do you have to accommodate those improvements into everyday routine. This makes for lasting change.

Outpatient treatment may allow you to lead an otherwise normal life of work and leisure, and force you to confront problems at home or work as you get better. For example, if you see your therapist in the afternoon, you might discuss particular difficulties you have in meal preparation in the evening, then go home and put those difficulties into practice. This makes therapy very meaningful.

Inpatients

On the other hand some people simply cannot make such changes without actually being admitted to hospital. Inpatient treatment is advocated for people whose illnesses are particularly severe, where there are issues of medical risk, where there are additional emotional problems such as depression, where a patient's thoughts or feelings put them at risk of suicide, or where social issues at home require a change of environment. Some patients receive inpatient treatment because of geography. If your nearest specialist service is not commutable, it would be necessary to be admitted to hospital. Inpatient treatment has the advantage of providing a complete and comprehensive package of emotional and physical care, 24 hours a day and seven days a week. Skills in management of medical complications can be particularly well-honed.

The support and encouragement of other patients can be tremendously healing. On the other hand, they can bring out the worst in you, as well as the best. This may vary on a unit from day to day, and is particularly pertinent for men with eating disorders. Being the only man on an inpatient unit can sometimes be difficult. On the other hand, gender is not as significant as other factors. An empathic, healing environment is far more important than whether your therapist is a man or a woman. Nonetheless, ensuring an inpatient unit has experience of treating men can be important.

Daypatients

A compromise between outpatient and inpatient treatment is the innovative approach of day-patient treatment. Day patients can offer the best of all worlds. Many day-patient units operate from 9 am to 5 pm throughout the working week. My own unit offers even longer hours, with the opportunity to attend hospital for breakfast, lunch and supper before returning home. This allows for more of the comprehensive support provided in inpatient treatment, but also keeps you in touch with your home life.

Our research has shown that day-patient treatment is effective even in severe cases, and rates of recovery are just as fast as for inpatients. Unfortunately, accessing day-patient treatment programmes is not always easy, not least because of the practical requirement that the unit be commutable from where you reside.

Medical wards

For some men with severe medical complications of their body image disorder, it is necessary to receive treatment on a medical ward. Guidelines for the treatment of eating disorders recommend that every region should have identified a physician with special expertise in eating disorders. Some of the physical complications of eating disorders can be quite complex. Such experts have the intellect to manage complex physical conditions, but also the wisdom to employ that intellect judiciously.

In very extreme cases, the effects of starvation on your mind may prevent you from reasoning, remembering or thinking. In a very few instances, people who have lost touch with reality may refuse life-saving treatment. When you are at 'death's door' from starvation, it can come as a relief to have responsibility taken over by someone else. This is a rare eventuality.

Summary

1   Find a sympathetic family doctor by shopping around, talking to other people with eating disorders and drawing on personal experience.
2   The family doctor is crucial in co-ordinating care and referring you to an appropriate agency.
3   Accessing specialist services can be tricky. The more you are informed about the process through self-help organisations such as Beat, the UK eating disorder association, the more likely you will succeed.
4   There are many different therapies for eating disorders, but the best of them combine a non-dogmatic approach with the requirement of addressing thoughts and behaviours together.
5   Treatments only addressing behaviours are unlikely to produce lasting change. Treatments only addressing thoughts are sterile.
6   You will be gratified by therapists who do not ask you to change behaviours, but the best forms of therapy are challenging, and may make you feel uncomfortable at times. That is why it is so important you find someone you trust.
7   Treatments are variously administered on an outpatient, daypatient and inpatient basis.
8   For some men with eating disorders, gender of therapist is relevant, but sincerity, empathy and understanding are more important than gender.

Chapter 19

Stage 7: Remaining well – sadder and wiser

This chapter is all about relapse prevention. We look at what is going to keep you on the straight and narrow, and the common mistakes people make that cause them to relapse into their old bad habits. Once you have reached a stage of recovery, you can begin to take stock. If your problem has been one of over-exercise or muscle dysmorphia, you may be beginning to broaden your life away from the rigid prison of compulsive over-exercise. If you have achieved weight restoration away from anorexia nervosa, you will experience clarity of thought and strength of body. If you are no longer binge eating, your self-esteem will be growing. Along with all these positives there may also be some negatives. Go back to your cost-benefit analysis of recovery, described in Stage 2 (Chapter 14). Does it still seem accurate?

For example, it is not uncommon to pass through a period of brief melancholy as you take stock. A host of authentic emotions can be experienced – all the feelings you have been artificially subduing through your illness. For some people, this is the period at which professional psychotherapy can be particularly helpful. Where the emotions are overwhelming, disabling and persistent, then there may be the need for more professional help. But it is far more common to experience the early stages of recovery simply as becoming sadder and wiser.

Remaining well depends on relapse prevention. Whilst most people with body image disorders make a full recovery, a significant minority have a tendency to relapse in response to future stress. It is almost inevitable that you will have the odd bad day, when some of the old behaviours rear their ugly heads. The difference between people who relapse and people who don't is not the emergence of these bad days, but how you react to them. The biggest causes of relapse are:

- setting yourself an impossibly high standard
- beating yourself up over your failure to maintain that standard.

If you have a bad Wednesday, you can dust yourself down and start Thursday with new enthusiasm. Or you can use Wednesday as an excuse to indulge your disorder. We see the same pattern in people with alcohol problems. Alcoholics frequently 'fall off the wagon', but it is the ability to get back on it again that determines long-term success or failure.

Forewarned is forearmed

By now you will have completed several months of diaries charting your behaviours. Those diaries contain everything you need to be forewarned and forearmed. From past experience, what are the signs that something is going wrong again? The answer will be different in every case. Perhaps you begin to distance yourself from old friends and go to the gym every day rather than thrice a week. Perhaps you start to exclude breakfast from your diet. Perhaps you convince yourself you have to go on the latest faddy diet.

Work out in advance what warning signs you will use to tell yourself you may be relapsing. Some of my patients have found it helpful to think of this in terms of traffic lights, with amber signs and red signs. For most men with eating disorders, a decision to avoid dieting is the single most important issue. For men with problems of compulsive exercise, ensuring at least three days free of exercise per week is a protective step.

Plan of attack

Next, work out in advance *exactly* what you will do if you score an amber or red light. Don't think in vague terms. Write it down. For example, if you are beginning to abuse exercise again, you may decide to go 'cold turkey' and stay away from the gym altogether for two weeks. If you are getting binge feelings, you may decide to automatically introduce an extra snack.

I find that most of my patients know exactly what they should be doing in these circumstances, but struggle to put it into practice. That is why you should construct your relapse prevention strategy while things are going well, not when they are going badly. You may find it helpful to recruit a buddy such as a friend or family member. First, you might give them permission to tell you if they think things are starting to unravel. It is often more immediately apparent to the buddy than the patient. Second, they can help you implement your plan. If you lack the motivation yourself, you can at least draw on them for motivation.

Fight the power

Finally, think of all the things that might tip you over the edge: family Christmases, drinking too much alcohol, splitting up with a partner, weight gain, conflict at work. Make sure you think through the possible scenarios. Visualise them. Now work out a plan of campaign. For instance, if you always take a turn for the worse after family get-togethers, make sure you have some stress-busting strategies for coping.

Summary

Everything you need for relapse prevention is contained in the diary work you have already completed. The biggest mistake is to wait for the relapse, catastrophise it and then slowly sink back into your old ways. Instead, you should be fully prepared for bad days, have a clear stratagem for managing them and then be prepared to implement this.

Chapter 20

Conclusion

The advantages of giving up your illness far outweigh the disadvantages. Only you can make that decision for yourself, but I hope that this book may assist you. I began this book by describing *The Invisible Man* as the first step in a longer journey. Now determine your next step.

John F Morgan
October 2007
www.psychiatry-uk.org

Resources

Books

The Adonis Complex: The Secret Crisis of Male Body Obsession, Harrison G. Pope, Katharine A. Phillips, Roberto Olivardia and Roberto Olivar, 2002, New York, Simon & Schuster. The authors provide a powerful account of muscle dysmorphia, which they have nicknamed 'the Adonis complex'. They write with the authority of leading researchers in their field, but with a lightness of touch that particularly elucidates the cultural background to bigorexia.

Anorexia and Bulimia in the Family – One Parent's Practical Guide to Recovery, Gráinne Smith, 2003, Chichester, Wiley. This book provides an invaluable insight for families of people with eating disorders. Written by a mother whose daughter has an eating disorder, it tells the story of Gráinne Smith and her daughter, including onset, symptoms, and the challenges that may face the family. The effects on family life are described, with practical tips for seeking help.

Anorexia Nervosa. A Survival Guide for Families, Friends and Sufferers, Janet Treasure, 1997, London, Brunner-Routledge. This book gives a clear description of the nature of the illness. It provides guidance and information for friends and carers, as well as the person with the illness.

Boys Get Anorexia Too – Coping with Male Eating Disorders in the Family, Jenny Langley, 2005, Bristol, Lucky Duck Publishing. The author writes from the experience of her son's anorexia nervosa at the age of 12, though now recovered. She provides not only a narrative of her experience, but also practical guidance for other parents. She now uses her experience to run a successful carers' support group and website (see below).

Bulimia Nervosa and Binge-Eating: A Guide to Recovery, Peter J. Cooper, 1993, London, Constable and Robinson. This book provides a description of the illness, an explanation of mechanisms that perpetuate the illness, descriptions of the medical complications and evaluation of all the treatments available. It includes a very practical self-help guide, offering a step-by-step programme to recovery. Like *Getting Better Bit(e) by Bit(e)* and *Overcoming Binge Eating*, this book is recommended as a first step towards recovery.

Fit to Die: Men and Eating Disorders, Anna Paterson, 2004, Bristol, Lucky Duck Publishing. The book conveys the growing cultural pressures that men are now experiencing with body image, and provides some practical guidance on recovery.

Getting Better Bit(e) by Bit(e), U. Schmidt and J. Treasure, 1993, Hove, Psychology Press. This popular and evidence-based guide combines cognitive and behavioural approaches, and is shown to be effective in self-help or guided self-help of bulimia nervosa. Using the self-help guide lessens demand for therapy and is recommended at an early stage in the 'stepped care' approach to bulimia.

Making Weight: Men's Conflicts with Food, Weight, Shape and Appearance, Arnold Andersen, Leigh Cohn and Tom Holbrook, 2000, Carlsbad, CA, Gurze Books. Written by some of the leading experts on male eating disorders, this book provides a fascinating and scientific narrative-based account of male body image problems.

Manhood – An Action Plan for Changing Men's Lives, S. Biddulph, 2002, Stroud, Hawthorn Press. A clever yet practical guide to issues of masculinity in the modern world.

Overcoming Binge Eating, Christopher G. Fairburn, 1995, New York, Guilford Press. A comprehensive account of the problem and treatment. Part Two of the book is a self-help programme based on strong evidence. Designed to be used on its own or in conjunction with therapy, it gives guidance on overcoming binge eating, maintaining control and relapse prevention.

Weblinks

The following weblinks refer principally to organisations that operate in the UK. There are equivalents to each in most other countries.

Beat (beating eating disorders)
www.b-eat.co.uk/Home
Beat is the principal UK charity for eating disorders. Its website is one of the best sources of information about the main eating disorders, including

the problems facing men and boys. Details of youth and adult telephone helplines are provided and there is considerable information about self-help and support groups. Contact with Beat is strongly recommended for men with eating disorders and their families. So helpful is the organisation that I donate a portion of this book's royalties to it.

Boy Anorexia
www.boyanorexia.com
Jenny Langley's informative website on anorexia nervosa in boys, in association with her helpful book, *Boys Get Anorexia Too*.

Male Health
http://www.malehealth.co.uk/
Male Health is a site with fast, free independent health information for men of all ages.

Men's Health Forum
www.menshealthforum.org.uk/
Men's Health Forum has a selection of health related information for men.

Royal College of Psychiatrists
www.rcpsych.ac.uk/mentalhealthinformation/mentalhealthproblems/eating disorders.aspx
The Royal College of Psychiatrists' website includes useful information on eating disorders.

Something Fishy
www.something-fishy.org
Something Fishy is an American website with emphasis on the patient's perspective and the emotional issues underlying the disorders. There are practical tips, motivational aids and suggestions for work on self-esteem and body image.

Survivors
http://www.survivorsuk.org/
Survivors provide information, support and counselling for men in the UK who have been raped or sexually abused.

References

British Medical Association Board of Science and Education (2002) *Drugs in Sport: The Pressure to Perform*, London: British Medical Association.

Bruch, H. (1978) *The Golden Cage*, Cambridge MA: Harvard University Press, p. 12.

Byron, George Gordon (1973) *Byron's Letters and Journals*, ed. Leslie A. Marchand, 12 vols, London: John Murray.

Choi, P. Y. and Pope, H. G. Jr (1994) Violence toward women and illicit androgenic-anabolic steroid use, *Annals of General Psychiatry* 6: 21–25.

Clare, A. (2000) *On Men: Masculinity in Crisis*, London: Chatto and Windus.

Crisp, A. H. (1995) *Anorexia Nervosa: Let Me Be*, Hove: Psychology Press.

DuRant, R. H., Rickert, V. I., Ashworth, C. S., Newman, C. and Slavens, G. (1993) Use of multiple drugs among adolescents who use anabolic steroids, *New England Journal of Medicine* 328: 922–926.

Copperman, J. (2000, 14 February) *Eating Disorders in the United Kingdom: Review of the Provision of Health Care Services for Men with Eating Disorders* (http://www.b-eat.co.uk/AboutEatingDisorders/Mengeteatingdisorderstoo, accessed October 1 2007).

Elwin, M. (1962) *Lord Byron's Wife*, London: John Murray.

Garner, D. M. and Garfinkel, P. E. (1980) Sociocultural factors in the development of anorexia nervosa, *Psychological Medicine* 10: 647–656.

Malone, D. A. Jr, Dimeff, R. and Lombardo, J. A. (1995) Sample BRH. Psychiatric effects and psychoactive substance use in anabolic-androgenic steroid users, *Clinical Journal of Sports Medicine* 5: 25–31.

Miller, W. R. and Rollnick, S. (2002) *Motivational Interviewing: Preparing People for Change*, New York: Guilford Press.

Morgan, J. F. (2000) From Charles Atlas to the Adonis complex – fat is more than a feminist issue, *Lancet* 356: 1372–1373.

Morgan, J. F., Key, A. and Lacey, J. H. (1998) Gender issues in the management of multi-impulsive bulimia, *International Journal of Eating Disorders* 24: 107–109.

Morgan, J. F. and Lacey, J. H. (1999) Scratching and fasting: a study of pruritus and weight restoration in anorexia nervosa, *British Journal of Dermatology* 140: 453–456.

Morgan, J. F., Lacey, J. H. and Reid, F. (1999) Anorexia nervosa: changes in sexuality during weight restoration, *Psychosomatic Medicine* 61: 541–545.

Morgan, J. F., Lacey, J. H., Murphy, H. and Conway, G. (2005) Long-term psychological outcome for adults with congenital adrenal hyperplasia: cross-sectional survey, *British Medical Journal* 330: 340–341.

Morton, R. (1694) *Phthisiologia: Or, a Treatise of Consumptions*, translated from the original. London, The Prince's Arms in St Paul's Churchyard: Smith and Walford.

National Institute for Health (1985) Health implications of obesity, *NIH Consensus Statement* 5 (9): 1–7.

Pope, H. G. and Katz, D. L. (1994) Psychiatric and medical effects of anabolic androgenic steroid use. A controlled study of 160 athletes, *Archives of General Psychiatry* 51: 375–382.

Russell, G. (1999) Bulimia nervosa: an ominous variant of anorexia nervosa, *Psychological Medicine*, 9 (3): 429–448.

Silverman, J. A. (1995) History of anorexia nervosa, in K. D. Brownell and C. G. Fairburn (eds) *Eating Disorders and Obesity*, New York: Guilford Press.

Slater, E. and Roth, M. (1969) Personality deviations and neurotic disorders, in E. Slater and M. Roth (eds) *Clinical Psychiatry*, 3rd edn, London: Bailliere, Tindall and Cassell, p. 143.

Thiblin, I., Lindquist, O. and Rajs, J. (2000) Cause and manner of death among users of anabolic androgenic steroids, *Journal of Forensic Sciences* 45 (1).

Wadsworth, M., Butterfield, W. and Blaney, R. (1971) *Health and Sickness: The Choice of Treatment*, London: Tavistock.

Wason, P. C. (1971) Natural and contrived experience in a reasoning problem, *Quarterly Journal of Experimental Psychology* 23: 63–71.

Whytt, R. (1764) *Observation on the Nature, Causes and Cures of those Disorders which have been commonly called nervous, Hypochondriac or Hysteric to which are prefixed some remarks on the Sympathy of the Nerves*, Edinburgh: Balfour.

Index